CONCILIUM

CONCILIUM 2002/5

THE RIGHTS OF WOMEN

Edited by

The Concilium Foundation

SCM Press · London

Published by SCM Press, 9–17 St Albans Place, London N1 0NX

ISBN 0 334 03071 4

Printed by Biddles Ltd, Guildford and King's Lynn

Concilium Published February, April, June, October
December

Contents

A Woman's Right to Not Being Straight (El Derecho a no ser Derecha): On Theology, Church and Pornography

Documentation
Recent Notifications on the Works of Reinhard Messner, Jacques Dupuis and Marciano Vidal

I. Women's Rights as Human Rights in a Global Context

The Rights of Women and Human Rights: Achievements and Contradictions

EVELYN A. KIRKLEY

It would seem self-evident that women's rights are human rights. Yet through centuries of global patriarchy and androcentrism, men have been considered the generic human and women derivative and subsidiary, 'misbegotten males' in Thomas Aquinas' famous phrase. In societies with strictly defined gender roles, it may be questioned if women deserve the same rights as men. Even in feminist circles, this issue has been controversial, in debates between essentialism vs. constructivism. Are women truly the same as men? Are their needs and rights identical? Some feminists respond that women deserve different rights to overcome the debilitating effects of patriarchy. Others argue that rights must be tailored to women's differences from men, in areas such as health care. Other feminists strongly disagree, asserting that special rights reinforce women's subordinate status. Moreover, how are women's rights affected by differences in nationality, class, race, ethnicity, sexual orientation, and other variables?

These questions arise when considering women's rights as human rights in a global theological context. They have no easy answers, beyond the fact that women are, strangely enough, human. Nonetheless, rights language has been a staple of the movement for women's equality inside Christian churches. Asserting women's equal rights with men based on their common humanity has led to significant progress for women in Christian history. Movements for women's acceptance as monastics, mystics, and priests are predicated on assertions of women's right to these roles. Yet while the women's rights movement in Christian churches has undoubtedly resulted in enormous strides, these accomplishments may be problematic. Achievements are often accompanied by ambivalence and contradiction, raising additional questions about the adequacy of rights language. Yet if accomplishment contains seeds of contradiction, contradictions can in turn lead to the possibility of further achievement.

Below is my non-exhaustive, idiosyncratic 'Top Ten' list of the most important accomplishments in the women's rights movement in Christian history and the contradictions they provoke. These are snapshots of individuals and groups that have revolutionized Christianity by advocating women's rights as human rights:

1. Perpetua († 202–3)

An early Christian martyr, this wealthy Roman matron was murdered for her faith in Carthage, North Africa. She demonstrated courage during her execution, rearranging her dishevelled clothes and hair after being gored by wild cows to die with dignity. She rejected traditional roles of daughter, wife, and mother and asserted her right to freedom in Christ. She chose martyrdom rather than subject herself to Roman household norms. Perpetua's story is told in the first person, raising the possibility that it is one of the earliest Christian documents authored by a woman.

Lurid, sensational, her story was widely preached and became well known precisely because she was a woman. Women were considered too emotionally weak and physically frail to sacrifice their lives. Perpetua demonstrated that women did possess the strength, faith, and personal fortitude to endure martyrdom. The contradiction is that she was stripped of her femaleness in the process. In a vision she saw herself as a male warrior for Christ, naked, oil rubbed into her muscles to prepare for battle against evil. Only as a spiritual transvestite could she demonstrate her faith and enter the arena of her death. Her femaleness was erased, either by herself or the author of her story. She became a non-woman, impossible for ordinary women to emulate without similarly shedding their sex. She was heroic despite her femaleness, not because of it.

2. Beguines (12th-14th centuries)

A widespread popular movement, the Beguines were groups of women who lived together in cities of present-day Belgium, France, and Germany. They committed themselves to poverty, simplicity, charity, piety, and chastity. Chastity did not mean they never married; some were married and lived separately from their husbands by mutual agreement, while others were single or widowed. Without formally adopting a rule, they created their own self-sufficient, autonomous households engaged in service to the poor. Supporting themselves as teachers, nurses, gardeners, and makers of cloth and lace, they contributed to the growing market economy of mediaeval Europe. They were particularly devoted to the passion of Christ in the eucharist; they sought to imitate Jesus' suffering through fasting, visions, and stigmata.

The Beguines formed uniquely female Christian communities, asserting their right to forge an alternative to cloistered religious orders and secular life. They demonstrated women's ability to create a religious movement apart from the church, to sustain themselves by their own labour. The contradiction is that they were perceived as a threat by church officials, beyond clergy control and therefore suspect. The Beguines did not conform to existing categories of female lay or religious piety and thus they were curtailed. In 1233, they were recognized semi-officially by the pope, which brought them under greater clerical supervision. They were accused of heresy for their mystical practices and attacked for their criticism of the church's wealth. Their autonomy over, the movement declined and within a century was nearly extinct.

3. Julian of Norwich (?1343–?1413)

Julian was an anchorite or solitary monastic who lived in a cell attached to a church in Norwich, England. Little is known of her biography. Her piety was well known, however, and she attracted visits from pilgrims. Her writings indicate she was well read, although she confessed to little formal education. In *The Revelations of Divine Love,* also called *Showings,* she described and interpreted sixteen visions in exquisite, allegorical detail. Her visions focussed on the Trinity, humanity and suffering of Christ, and the motherhood of God. She depicted the Second Person of the Trinity as maternal. Through the incarnation Christ had generative power like a mother. Christ nurtured and protected his children from harm as a mother. Jesus provided food for humanity from his own body and blood as a mother provides milk from her own breast. As mother Jesus loved her children unconditionally, disciplined them when necessary, and sustained them through her strength.

Julian's achievement is her exegesis of Christ as mother through her visions. Although her characterization of Christ with female traits was not unprecedented, it was highly unusual, especially because written within the orthodox context of an anchorite attached to the church. She developed a theology of Jesus' motherhood more thoroughly than any other mediaeval theologian. She demonstrated that women are capable of theological and mystical reflection. Her contradiction is that her ideas were not developed by subsequent theologians, and so her work was virtually lost for generations. Ignored by male theologians, her ideas disappeared from the fabric of orthodoxy. Her visions were largely unknown until recovered by twentieth-century feminist theologians.

4. Sor Juana Ines de la Cruz (1648–95)

A nun in Mexico City, Sor Juana was the first theologian of the Western hemisphere, the so-called New World. Highly erudite compared with any man of her day, she possessed a library of thousands of volumes, was an accomplished musician and poet, and convened a salon from her monastic cell that made her a favourite of the viceroy and his court. In 1690 she became embroiled in a dispute between the local bishop and archbishop and wrote her sole published work *Reply to Sor Philothea*. In it she defended women's rights to theological education by lauding biblical heroines Miriam, Deborah, Esther, Mary, and Phoebe and by stressing Paul's instructions that older women teach younger ones. She also emphasized the benefits educated women would bring to church and society. After the *Reply* was published, the archbishop was furious and ordered her books, scientific instruments, and musical instruments confiscated. Her salon was closed, she went into seclusion, and she wrote no further works for the public.

Sor Juana's accomplishment is certainly her passionate assertion of women's right to education in the Bible, Christian history, and doctrine. Women must be educated to fulfill their Christian responsibility to teach others. Like Julian, she demonstrated that women were as capable theologians as men. The contradiction is that like the Beguines, Sor Juana's insights were ignored and suppressed by church authorities, and she was lost from history until recent years. Her challenge to the church was too threatening, and she was silenced.

5. Elizabeth Cady Stanton (1815–1902)

Born in upstate New York, Cady Stanton lived most of her life in the northeastern United States. Daughter of a judge, she received better than the usual education for a girl, but recalled throughout her life her father's disappointment that she was not a son. She married reformer and abolitionist Henry Stanton and on their wedding trip attended an anti-slavery conference in London. There she and other women delegates were stunned to discover that they were not allowed to vote or sit on the main floor of the assembly. Cady Stanton determined to devote her life to women's rights, and in 1848 she called the first US women's rights conference in Seneca Falls, New York. She became the primary theorist of the movement, focussing on women's right to enfranchisement, education, property ownership, and divorce. She based her defence of women's rights on their status as tax-paying citizens under the US Constitution.

Towards the end of her life, she became convinced that Christianity and the Bible were the primary obstacles to women's full human rights. In 1895 and 1898, she published *The Woman's Bible*, a two-volume commentary on biblical passages dealing with women. She wrote over half the commentaries herself, with help from a committee of other feminists. She condemned the Bible for preaching that women were created after men and caused the fall of humanity, blaming Christianity for women's second-class status and internalized oppression. Yet she praised biblical women like Esther, Vashti, and Jael who demonstrated strength, courage, and quick thinking. In so far as the Bible encouraged women to think for themselves and challenge the status quo, she argued, it was valuable. But women must read the Bible for themselves and not allow husbands or pastors to tell them what it said. Women had the God-given responsibility to think for themselves and act upon their convictions, not merely parrot what they were taught.

Cady Stanton was a classic liberal feminist thinker, rooting her arguments in Enlightenment principles of equality, justice, and individualism. She made the revolutionary argument that not only *may* women interpret the Bible, but they *must* interpret it. Women must develop their own faith. The contradiction is that like the Beguines and Sor Juana, Cady Stanton and *The Woman's Bible* were vilified, not only by clerical leaders, but by the lay Christian community and her closest friends and co-workers. At a 1896 women's rights convention, delegates explicitly disassociated themselves from the project, thus rejecting the founder of their movement. Acclaimed solely by a small group of atheists and agnostics, Cady Stanton's ideas were too threatening for general consumption.

6. Women's Ordination Conference/
7. Evangelical and Ecumenical Women's Caucus

Founded in 1975, incorporated in 1977, and with its headquarters in Fairfax, Virginia, the Women's Ordination Conference (WOC) is a US-based Catholic organization that works with global movements for women's ordination as priests and bishops in the Roman Catholic Church. Committed to justice, equality, and inclusivity in ecclesiastical structures, the WOC strives to end all forms of discrimination and support women's calls to ministry. The WOC has met with bishops, confronted clerical leaders including the pope, and picketed episcopal meetings to protest sexism in the church. Along with activism, it conducts surveys of lay Catholics on the issue of women's ordination, builds coalitions with other Catholic groups, and leads educational programmes on biblical, theological, and historical foundations for women's ordination. It maintains strong relationships with theologians and the press.

Founded in 1974, comprised of Protestant women and men, the Evangelical and Ecumenical Women's Caucus (EEWC) advocates women's ordination and exercise of pastoral leadership, use of inclusive language in worship, and biblical feminism. The EEWC asserts that the Bible affirms equality between women and men and that Christian churches have promoted male dominance and female passivity. Organized into local chapters, regional events, and national conferences, it is inclusive of gender, race, sexual orientation, age, disability, economic status, and religious affiliation. It sponsors educational programmes for Christian feminists to learn from, network with, and encourage one another.

The accomplishments of WOC and EEWC are threefold: they provide a pulpit from which women and men proclaim their conviction that God calls women to priestly and pastoral ministry; they create community for thousands to advocate justice and equality without leaving the church; and they educate the wider Christian community on sexism in the church. Both WOC and EEWC stress education and consciousness-raising and are international in membership. They are too large and well organized to be suppressed or silenced. Yet the contradiction is the weak impact these groups have had on ecclesiastical and denominational authorities. They have not influenced decisions in the hierarchy. Despite popular support, large memberships, and commitment to remain within the church, they are more gadflies than effective agents of change.

8. Woman-church movement /
9. Re-Imagining Conference

Beginning in the 1980s, Christian feminists, male and female, have gathered for worship and to nurture their spirituality through a loosely organized movement called women-church. Small groups meet in homes, churches, and other places to experiment and experience a spirituality that feels more authentic than androcentric Christian worship. It may include dance, art, chanting, or other artistic forms. Women-church is ecumenical and at times interfaith. It aims to nurture women's voices in theology and worship, assuming free expression is seldom possible in established Christian traditions. Men participate in women-church, although most leaders and participants are women. They are not schismatic; they want to maintain their relationships to established churches and transform them through their presence. They view women-church as separate space within the church in which women can find their voices.

An international, three-day kind of women-church gathering occurred in 1993 with the Re-Imagining Conference in Minneapolis, Minnesota. Organized to celebrate the mid-point of the World Council of Churches 'Ecumenical Decade: Churches in Solidarity with Women' from 1988–98, it featured speakers from ten denominations and twelve countries. Primary sponsors were the Presbyterian Church, USA and the United Methodist Church. Over two thousand people attended, mostly women, a third of them clergy, from different ethnic background and sexual orientations. The conference included worship, workshops, and keynote presentations. Through singing, dance, art, and drama, it aimed to create a Christian community, safe space for participants to affirm their understandings of the sacred. Worship included invocations to Sophia, the biblical image of wisdom, and a ritual of celebration with milk and honey.

The accomplishment of women-church and the Re-Imagining Conference is their courageous trail-blazing of new forms of Christian ritual and community. Asserting women's right to create their own spirituality, they have pioneered new definitions of church from a feminist perspective. Yet this achievement exacted a price. Both movements have been attacked as being un-Christian, anti-Christian, or pagan for their use of inclusive language and willingness to adapt traditional forms of worship. They have been criticized for promoting lesbianism and a feminist political agenda. The Re-Imagining Conference provoked outrage among more conservative Presbyterians and Methodists. One organizer lost her job, and others felt their positions threatened when their attendance was discovered.

10. Global feminist theologians

In the last twenty years, African and African-American theologians like Jacquelyn Grant, Katie Cannon, Emilie Townes, Delores Williams, and

Mercy Amba Oduyoye; Latina theologians such as María Pilar Aquino and Ada Maria Isasi-Diaz; and Asian theologians Chung Hyun Kyung and Kwok Pui-Lan have revolutionalized Christian feminist theology. Prior to their work, feminist theologians, predominantly Anglo, middle class, and North American, seldom addressed issues of race, class, and ethnicity. The global theologians, some self-designated womanist, mujerista, or minjung, have asserted that race and class must be intersected with gender or else inadvertently support racism and classism. They bring a global social consciousness to feminist theology by raising issues of poverty, health care, economic self-sufficiency, contraception, and domestic and sexual abuse and connecting them with Christianity. While stressing the importance of tradition and community, they challenge societal structures like capitalism and ecclesiastical hierarchy that enable the status quo to maintain power. They speak for the voiceless, those without advantages of money, education, or the right skin colour, ordinary women who struggle to feed their children. While these theologians differ from one another at times, they have provided a critical corrective to feminist theology. By lifting up lives of women who lack access to power and legal rights, they have connected the need for women's rights on a global scale with Christian theology.

These theologians assert women's right to do theology outside the Western, Anglo mainstream. They revise not only the content of Christian theology, but also its methodology. They challenge theologians and church leaders to address more adequately the social and political needs of ordinary Christian women. They expand the Christian tradition while remaining faithful to it. The contradictions are less clear. Will other theologians adopt their new methodologies? Will church leaders respond to issues they raise? It is yet too early to tell.

Conclusion

It is evident from the above that women have achieved much in Christian history by asserting their right to the same roles as men, as martyrs, monastics, mystics, activists, theologians, and church leaders. Yet these accomplishments often contain one of two contradictions: the women are either suppressed by church authorities or exceptionalized, treated as anomalous, their unusual deeds unattainable by ordinary women. Either way their radicalism is controlled, their challenge to religious structures downplayed, their conformation to established gender roles stressed.

Along with these achievements and contradictions, rights language is itself problematic. As feminist theorists like Elizabeth Fox Genovese, Sylvia Ann Hewlett, and Mary Daly have noted, rights language can penalize women by presuming they are entitled to rights men possess and no more. Based on Enlightenment thinking and the legal system, the language of rights obviates the possibility that women have special needs, privileges, and protections inaccessible to men. Rights language assumes there is one playing field and that women will be equal to men by granting them identical rights. Rights language assumes there is a discrete body of politically, legally, or ecclesiastically defined rights and focusses on the individual as sole possessor of these rights without a systemic or collective dimension.

Yet what other starting point is there for asserting justice and equality for women? It just may not be the ending point.

Select bibliography

María Pilar Aquino, *Our Cry for Life: Feminist Theology from Latin America*, Maryknoll, NY: Orbis 1993.

Katie G. Cannon, *Black Womanist Ethics*, Atlanta, GA: Scholars 1988.

Anne E. Carr, *Transforming Grace: Christian Tradition and Women's Experience*, New York: Continuum 1996.

Elizabeth A. Clark and Herbert Richardson (eds), *Women and Religion: The Original Sourcebook of Women in Christian Thought*, revised and expanded edition, New York: HarperCollins 1996.

Anne M. Clifford, *Introducing Feminist Theology*, Maryknoll, NY: Orbis 2001.

Virginia Fabella and Mercy Amba Oduyoye (eds), *Third World Women Doing Theology*, Maryknoll, NY: Orbis 1988.

Jacquelyn Grant, *White Women's Christ and Black Women's Jesus: Feminist Christology and Womanist Response*, Atlanta, GA: Scholars 1989.

Ada Maria Isasi-Diaz, *En La Lucha: In the Struggle: Elaborating a Mujerista Theology*, Minneapolis, MN: Fortress 1993.

Barbara J. MacHaffie, *Her Story: Women in Christian Tradition*, Philadelphia: Fortress 1986.

Elizabeth A. Petroff (ed.), *Medieval Women's Visionary Literature*, New York: Oxford 1986.

Rosemary Radford Ruether, *Women-Church: Theology and Practice of Feminist Liturgical Communities*, San Francisco: Harper and Row 1985.

Carl J. and Dorothy Schneider, *In Their Own Right: The History of American Clergywomen*, New York: Crossroad 1997.

Delores S. Williams, *Sisters in the Wilderness: The Challenge of Womanist God-Talk*, Maryknoll, NY: Orbis 1993.

Women's Rights as Human Rights in a Global Context, Globalization and the Violation of Wo/men's Rights

Critical theory and feminist liberation ethics emphasize actual problems in social life that must be solved.[1] It is by analysing real problems and people's real lives that we gain knowledge about different levels and kinds of justice. One major voice in feminist liberation ethics is Beverly Harrison. She makes use of critical theory and asks theologians and ethicists to equip themselves with relevant social knowledge that will enable Christian social ethics to maintain a consistent effort to grapple with economic justice.[2] In spite of much criticism against critical theory's ambition to transform society in directions of justice, a new lively discussion about critical theory has surfaced among feminists who hold on to the ambition of political philosophy to find a way ahead that is more just. Feminist liberation ethics maintain what may seem on the verge of being blasé, when they keep asking critical questions of those who are exploited; *gather the information, analyse it and act on it.* Feminist economist Julie A. Nelson asks the question: 'What would economic theory look like if the center issue was how to provide for basic need?'[3]

In this article I argue that feminist economists raise much the same issues on behalf of the poor as do liberation theologians. Eradication of poverty is a main task for international bodies, church and secular institutions alike. A great many strategies have failed to eradicate poverty. Justice is indeed not a strategy; it is merely another way to argue for a more equal distribution, and above all access to distributive mechanisms.. A feminist contribution to this endeavour could be to establish a bottom line for economic justice. Hopefully the weight of the argument will draw out new actors from economic theory.

I. Justice and welfare

1. Two economic traditions

Two major traditions exist in economic theory in relation to social values. Much in the tradition of Aristotle, a research project at the theological faculty at Uppsala University has looked at two major economic traditions: the engineering market economics way of doing economics and the ethical welfare way of doing economics.

The neo-classical/neo-liberal school of economics has been ardent in its efforts to disconnect itself from social sciences and social values. Nobel laureate Milton Friedman of the Chicago school of economics is one of the well-known leaders of the neo-liberal school. Neo-liberal market economics claim to be neutral to issues of value and ethics in the pursuit of utility maximization and prefer to relate to natural sciences in investigating the nature of the market. Since the market requires unlimited freedom its natural habitat is economic globalization.

The most well-known economist who continues to explore the justice and welfare aspects of economics is Nobel laureate Amartya Sen, who is a member of the International Association of Feminist Economics. Human beings are capable movers in their lives, can form their future and should be valued as autonomous subjects who deserve good and equal opportunities. Capabilities is the concept that Sen has developed to refer to the fact that everybody is a concrete other who, given the opportunity, is able to change her own life. Sen demands that politicians provide oil for the social machinery to support human capabilities. His thorough research of famines shows that good political foresight does prevent the disastrous consequences of famines.

2. Forms of poverty

Poverty takes many forms. It includes all kinds of deprivation: physical, psychological, biological, medical, educational, and spiritual. At a low estimate, the number of people who are deprived of the right to sustain their lives runs at about 1,200 million. This makes it one of the pressing issues of our times.

Six billion people live on the little planet earth, and by a small margin a majority of those people are women. Another majority of the earth's people are children and young people. By the most conservative estimates, 700 million people are starving. Many more people are malnourished. The richest 20% of people in the world consume 80% of the resources, while the poorest 20 % get a couple of per cents of the consumer goods.

Child mortality has declined, but every day 18,000 children under the age of five die from malnutrition and curable diseases. In the least developed countries, 109 children out of a thousand died at birth, compared to 13 out of a thousand in the industrial world. Of 100,000 women giving birth, 1,100 died in the least developed countries, compared to 30 in the industrial world.[4] Safe water is not available for about 1200 million people.[5] The mean for women's income in the world in 1997 was US$4.435 to men's US$8.587; in the OECD (Organization for Economic Co-operation and Development) men earn US$26.743 compared to women's US$14.165.[6] Many women work part time since they take care of households and hence work in the informal sector, so the figures are not easily comparable; but women consistently get less.

3. Situation of women

In the Nordic countries, 89% of women are in employment. This figure is calculated in relation to a 100% male work force. In neither case are as many women and men working, but it allows for comparisons of wages. Women earn consistently less than men and while the gap is least in the Nordic countries it is still considerable.

In Sweden, women earn around 72% of the wages men earn. When the figures are adjusted for part time work, age and number of years in the profession, women earn about 90% of the wages men earn.[7]

Since women are at the bottom of all available statistics, it makes sense to study women's situation. My claim is that it is a human right to be able to provide for one's own *basic human needs* and that this is a universal right which marks where economic theory and practice goes through the bottom line of any justice claims. It is simply unjust. The basic human needs of the poor must be prioritized in any ethical discourse about rights and justice. Basic human needs include safe water, food, shelter, basic education, basic health care and sanitation in a sustainable manner. Even though we need different amounts and styles of those items, they are necessities for everyone in some measure. I focus on the material needs, since they have universal features that can be used to establish universal normative ethics in economics, albeit that these arise from a micro rather than a macro economic perspective.

II. Feminist economics

1. Fallacy of misplaced concretness

Feminist economics is a newcomer on the tree of feminist theory, emerging in the early 1990s. Feminist economists come from all corners of economic theory but many are trained in the neo-classical school of economics. As feminists, many have seen the real live situation that causes many of the problems women face. They have found *the fallacy of misplaced concretness*[8] of economics offensive. Data arising from feminist economists in the South, such as Bina Agarwal, are pointing out how the deprivation of women systematically makes women poor and powerless. If women were granted the same rights as men when it comes to owning and using land in South Asia, they would be able to provide for themselves and their children and also get access to the political system.[9] Agarwal's critique concerns mainly political economy – a word seldom used any more – and how women's human rights are violated by patriarchal tradition, religion and culture. When and if women had the same rights and possibilities of accessing the market as men do, they would do as well as men. The profit or the salary women would receive would also benefit their children to a larger extent than men's income does. The figures differ in different countries and different circumstances but show consistently that women spend a greater portion of their income within the family than do men.[10]

Another poignant question that feminists ask concerns the *discipline* of economics *itself*. The theoretical complexity of economic models demands big computers to process the hypothetical questions, but are they connected to real-life issues? A strong critique against economic theory from feminists concerns the extent of autonomous non-connected theorizing that is paraded as hard objective science.[11] Tending to a household is a practical matter. Tending to the household of all God's people requires practical strategies rather than theoretical abstractions.

2. Scarcity and military spending

Scarcity is the ultimate problem and the pinnacle of economic theory and it is also the cause and foundation of poverty.[12] In fact economics is defined as the art of maintaining a household with scarce resources. Resources are scarce for many of us. They are particularly scarce when we consider all the things we want and may assume that we need. When we look at the global household, in some places there is extreme scarcity, while in other places there is extreme wealth. If the world was a common household and if resources to satisfy basic needs were redistributed to where they are needed, there would be no scarcity. This is a bold claim so here is some evidence.

Military spending is not the answer to the question directed to economic theory, but provides a good comparison. Through political decisions, the military is included in the national budget and takes money from common resources. Every year the world spends about 800 billion dollars for the military-industrial complex. It was hoped that this figure would decline with the abolition of the Soviet Union (remember!). Percentage-wise it may have, but due to recent events and the immense wealth of the US, the actual amount remains about the same and is increasing. United Nations Development Fund (UNDP) estimates that 40 billion dollars a year would make it possible to provide those needs for people who lack them today. In other words, a mere 5% of military spending every year would radically change the outlook of things for the poor.

III. Feminist liberation ethics

Economic globalization is commonly considered to be the cause of many social problems in the world today. Liberation theology in all its forms has the poor at heart, and feminist liberation ethics focusses on the oppression of women. How can feminist liberation ethics contribute to the analysis of economic globalization? My explorations concern how feminist liberation ethics can help to establish a bottom line for economic justice.

1. Challenges

Feminist liberation ethics undertakes the risky project of suggesting *universal norms*, but norms derived from the bottom up, rather than from the top down. I challenge economic theory to work harder with issues of economic justice.

Feminist liberation ethics aims, not to exclude theory, but to broaden the *complexity* and scope of the data included in reasoning processes concerning economic justice. Poor women's experience of economic deprivation can serve as a fruitful starting point to elaborate both the nature of poverty and the struggle against injustice. When looking at the most deprived people on earth, and while speaking to them and, most important of all when listening to them, it is hard to refute the fact that their voices carry a special weight that demands that they are given a particular epistemological privilege.

The notion of equality is key in the reasoning of feminist economists and, while keeping in mind the particular context of Christian feminist ethics, feminist liberation ethics can improve the argument for *equality*. The foundation of equality in Christian feminist ethics is based in contemporary feminist theory and the women's movement, both of which emphasize the importance of experience. Equality is also based in the biblical context where it is spelled out that humans are created in the image of God and that subjects are loved equally by God. This understanding of equality connects to value and disregards all differences as being secondary to our universal claims for equal human rights. It is time to own and put forth a total equality between all human persons and all children when it comes to value as founded and well-founded in Christian social ethics and religion. And to challenge other persuasions to do the same.

Oppression is a central issue for liberation theology, and feminists in the school of critical theory are carefully examining the tangibility of oppression. My claim is that the *bottom line* of economic justice in the global market economy, which is engulfed in neo-classic economics, must be that of establishing the right of every individual to sustain his or her life and have access to basic human needs in a sustainable manner.

2. What is justice?

Justice is a most precarious dream fostered by humanity. Justice is a vision akin to the vision of heaven: many have heard about it, read about it and longed for it, but no one has seen it. I want to explore economic justice from the perspective of poor women's real life experiences.

A major focus of economic justice discourse is distribution of resources. There are indeed a number of variables that are included to decide what would constitute a just distribution of resources, which most often tend to refer to a redistribution of resources by political decisions. Discussions about distributive justice generally assume that equal distribution is a just distribution. The objects to be distributed are (a) equal opportunities, (b) equal rights, (c) equal social goods. Since Amartya Sen raised the question *equality of what?*, [13] the intricacies of equality have been explored thoroughly.

A feminist economic justice discourse starts from the bottom where deprivation is the main issue. Choosing to focus on meeting basic human needs instead of an abstract notion of equal distribution will focus on the practice of basic justice.

Justice is the vehicle ethicists use to reason about distribution of resources, but levels of justice change all the time. There are situations when we can no longer find any traces of justice at all. The subject of economic justice in a feminist discourse starts with the least well off and views justice not as a state of things but as a process.

In order to improve economic justice data from all sciences and all human wisdom must be included as it appears. The hermeneutical spiral that feminists favour is a method for this enterprise. Openness, suspicion, epistemological privilege, historical consciousness, recognition of the entire human family, respect, mutual equality, the rainbow and more goes into this process to understand and improve justice. The hermeneutics of justice in feminist liberation ethics includes the question: who will profit from this order? Which in some way is a turn around of the Pareto optimal order, which requires that someone can improve his assets while no one else loses anything? In a world of unequal distribution, one may ask if there is really any point in worrying if the rich lose something, because the poor get something. Economics is supposedly a helpmate to accomplish other goals, i.e. to maximize individual utility in the market place. But the method has become the goal, not a vehicle for the common good or to better the situation of the poor.

Global market economy is distant from the single household economy, but the lives of individual people and the international market have become intrinsically intertwined and, therefore, it is an important task for ethics, economics and political philosophy to theorize on the conditions of the possibility to improve economic justice.

IV. Critical theory and feminist political philosophy

Feminists trying to improve the argument for basic justice do this from the perspective of oppression in its many varied forms. Oppression has five different faces according to Iris Marion Young. In her book *Justice and the Politics of Difference*[14] she makes an eloquent analysis of the five faces of oppression.

1. Exploitation

The old well-known subject of *exploitation* is a form of oppression that affects many people on the globe today. Feminists who connect to critical theory refer to a developed and changed Marxian analysis. While lacking analysis of gender or ethnicity, when it comes to exploitation, Marx's work still provides foundational insights. Modernity prides itself on the way facts are crucial to what is presented in analysis and much has changed since Marx started his prudent investigations of the actual problems from the perspective of the workers. As a matter of method, it is correct to assess that his views are now congruent with mainstream social sciences.

The crucial nature of exploitation is that profit is structurally and consistently transferred from the exploited to the exploiter. Feminists have carefully pointed out that exploitation does not affect all the exploited to the same degree; the exploitive mechanisms still apply. The other appearances of oppression are marginalization, powerlessness, violence and cultural imperialism.

In this way, Young accomplishes a pluralistic understanding of oppression that includes many of the issues that have given rise to disagreement about oppression. She recognizes the claim to be in an oppressed situation as valid for many peoples and groups. For those who focus on liberation from oppression it is imperative to the greatest extent possible not to fall in the same pit that you critique.

2. Redistribution

From the school of critical theory, recognition is the encompassing theme for oppression that Nancy Fraser uses in her work on political philosophy.[15] Fraser emphasizes that the major task of critical theory is to take on recognition and redistribution and use them both instead of presenting them as opposites. Feminist theory has developed a sophisticated diversity of oppressive contexts in the human family. A great many well-grounded claims to be liberated have been taken very seriously. Context and particularity are key concepts in how theorizing about universal norms have been dismounted. Fraser demands that difficulties pertaining to exploitation which requires redistribution and recognition (oppression that connects to connotations like gender, 'race' , sexual orientation and class) be included in order to get a handle on pressing issues and a way to discuss universal norms.

Among feminists of many kinds there is a clear commitment to the welfare state and its redistributive instruments that have worked well in Northern Europe. The kind of political economy that is featured in this part of the world has a fundamental strand of solidarity as its foundation.

In Northern Europe there exists some kind of social ethos that recognizes the concrete other as a person with the same needs and rights as everybody else. This view seem to be lost in the Christian right.

Redistribution is, however, not a question to be solved by economic theorists. Theirs is the task to improve theory to include those who are not even considered to be exploited. For neo-classical economics to participate in a post-Hobbe's society, the issue of economic justice for people who are equals, who are entitled to the same human rights in a globalized world, is a necessary subject matter. This is a universal norm.

V. Conclusion

1. Feminism and economic justice

A theory of economic justice developed by feminist ethicists must inevitably start with those who are destitute to the extent that they are not even considered for exploitation. To be cast into a category of people who do not even qualify for exploitation in economic terms constitutes an immediate threat to one's life. People who are starving display every characteristic of oppression imaginable. To begin with, they are the most downtrodden. They are also marginalized to the level of being invisible. At least 1200 million people are outside any political economy that would secure their daily bread by redistribution. The poor have very little power unless they get organized. Liberation theology originally didn't recognize that women are at the bottom of the relatively short span of poverty. A feminist theory of economic justice will always start in practice and always at the bottom, a far cry from a construction of perfect justice.

2. A challenge to neo-liberals

An issue for economic theory, if it were to find means to improve economic justice, is to ask how the market should/could become more accessible for the poor. Redistribution of resources is a task for political economy and politicians. But there must be something to redistribute. Accessibility to the market is a crucial concept in neo-classic economic theory. How can accessibility apply to the poor who are marginalized to extent of invisibility in the theory as it stands?

It is the task of feminist liberation ethics to keep asking what economic theory can contribute to improve economic justice. Poor women and other poor people are subjects in their own lives, with their own capabilities and an autonomous right to sustain their lives through their own efforts when they are able and willing to do so.

Notes

1. A special thanks to Dr Mary Condren, Dublin, Ireland for her reflections on this article.
2. Beverly Wildung Harrison, *Making the Connections* (ed) Carol Robb, Boston: Beacon Press 1985, p.55.
3. Julie A. Nelson, *Feminism, Objectivity & Economics*, New York: Routledge 1996, p.36.
4. Human Development Report 1998, New York: UNDP, table 12, pp.156–57.
5. Human Development Report 1996, New York: UNDP, table 5, pp.146–47.
6. Human Development Report 2000, New York: UNDP, p.164.
7. The World's Women, Trends and Statistics 1995, New York: UN, p.128.
8. Herman E. Daly and John B. Cobb, Jr., *For The Common Good*, Boston: Beacon Press 1989, pp.35–37. The expression *fallacy of misplaced concreteness* was developed by Alfred North Whitehead when he discussed economics and its prevalent tendency to draw conclusions from abstractions to real life. His notions have been developed by Julie A. Nelson.
9. Bina Agarwal, *A Field of Ones Own, Gender and Land Rights in South Asia*, Cambridge University Press 1994.
10. Ibid., pp. 28–29. Here Agarwal gives many references.
11. Sandra Harding, 'Can feminist thought make economics more objective' in *Feminist Economics*, 1995, Vol.1, No.1.
12. Whether or not it makes sense to talk about scarcity in a world of abundance is another pressing matter. For the poor it is an immediate reality.
13. Amartya Sen, *Inequality Reexamined*, New York Russell Sage Foundation, Oxford: Clarendon Press 1992.
14. Iris Marion Young, *Justice and the Politics of Difference*, Princeton: Princeton University Press 1990, pp.48–63.
15. Nancy Fraser, *Justice Interruptus. Critical reflections on the 'Postsocialist' condition'*, London, New York: Routledge 1997.

Between Women: Migrant Domestic Work and Gender Inequalities in the New Global Economy

RHACEL SALAZAR PARREÑAS

The South to North flow

Migrants without doubt have a new face. No longer do men who seek low-wage jobs in construction or heavy manufacturing lead the flow of workers from poorer to richer nations in the new global economy. With or without them, women relocate across nation-states and enter the global labour market independently. They respond to the high demand for low-wage domestic work in richer nations the world over. A South to North flow of domestic workers has emerged with women from Mexico and Central America moving into the households of working families in the United States; Indonesian women to richer nations in Asia and the Middle East; Sri Lanka women to Greece and the Middle East; Polish women to Western Europe; and Caribbean women to the United States and Canada.[1] In a much wider and greater scale, women from the Philippines also respond to the demand for migrant domestic workers. Providing their service in more than 160 countries, Filipino women are considered the domestic workers *par excellence* of globalization.[2] In Europe alone, a fairly large number of them work in the private households of middle to upper-income families in Great Britain, France, the Netherlands, Italy, Spain, and Greece.

In this article, I look at the South to North flow of migrant domestic workers and examine how processes of globalization reinforce relations of inequality among women. I do this by looking at the labour of caring for one's own family. By this I mean the labour of tending to the personal needs and well-being of individuals in the family. Despite the increase in women's labour market participation in both developing and advanced capitalist countries, the work of nurturing the family is still primarily relegated to women. Yet this burden is not a convenient platform for alliance among women, as it is a source of inequality between them.

To relieve the burden of housework, women rely on the commodification of this work and purchase the low-wage services of poorer women. And in our globalized society, it is migrant women workers from the South who are more and more freeing women in the North of this burden. Yet, this has significant consequences in respect of relations between women. The advancement of one group of women is at the cost of the disadvantage of another group of women, because in the process of freeing other women of this burden, migrant domestic workers from the South are usually denied the human right of caring for their own family. In this article, I unravel this paradoxical positioning of women so as to address its challenges to our efforts of building transnational feminist alliances in globalization.

I. Migrant domestic work and the international division of care work

At the same time that it remains the work of women, the labour of caring for the family continues to be a private and not a public responsibility.[3] To emphasize this point, I revisit my argument on the international transfer of care work, meaning the three-tier transfer of care among women in sending and receiving countries of migration.[4] Under this macro-process, class-privileged women pass down the care of their families to migrant domestic workers as migrant domestic workers simultaneously pass down the care of their own families – most of whom are left behind in the country of origin – to their relatives or sometimes even poorer women whom they hire as their own domestic workers.

1. The case of Carmen Ronquillo

The case of Carmen Ronquillo, a domestic worker in Rome, provides us with a good illustration of the international division of carework. Carmen is simultaneously a domestic worker for a professional woman in Rome and an employer of a domestic worker in the Philippines. Carmen describes her relationship to each one of these women:

When coming here, I mentally surrendered myself and forced my pride away from me to prepare myself. But I lost a lot of weight. I was not used to the work. You see, I had maids in the Philippines. I have a maid in the

Philippines that has worked for me since my daughter was born twenty-four years ago. She is still with me. I paid her 300 pesos before, and now I pay her 1000 pesos. I am a little bit luckier than others because I run the entire household. My employer is a divorced woman who is an architect. She does not have time to run her household so I do all the shopping. I am the one budgeting. I am the one cooking. [Laughs.] And I am the one cleaning too. She has a twenty-four and twenty-six year old. The older one graduated already and is an electrical engineer. The other one is taking up philosophy. They still live with her . . . She has been my only employer. I stayed with her because I feel at home with her.[5]

It is quite striking to observe the formation of parallel relationships of loyalty between Carmen (the employer) and her domestic in the Philippines and Carmen (the domestic) and her employer in Italy. Also striking is the fact that Carmen's domestic worker does exactly the same work that Carmen does for her own employer. Yet, more striking is the wide discrepancy in wages between Carmen and her own domestic worker.

Their wage differences illuminate the economic disparity among nations in transnational capitalism. A domestic worker in Italy such as Carmen could receive US$1000 a month for her labour. As Carmen describes,

I earn 1,500,000 lira (US$1000) and she pays for my benefits. On Sundays, I have a part-time. I clean her office in the morning and she pays me 300,000 lira (US$200). I am very fortunate because she always gives me my holiday pay in August and my thirteenth month pay in December. Plus, she gives me my liquidation pay at the end of the year.

Carmen's wages easily enable her to hire a domestic worker in the Philippines, who on average only earns what is the equivalent of $40 during the time of my interviews. Moreover, the domestic worker in the Philippines, in exchange for her labour, does not receive the additional work benefits that Carmen receives for the same labour.[6]

2. A gradational decline

Under the international division of care work, there is a gradational decline in the worth of care. As sociologist Barbara Rothman poignantly describes, 'When performed by mothers, we call this mothering . . .; when performed by hired hands, we call it unskilled.'[7] Commodified care work is not only low-paid work but declines in market value as it gets passed down the hierarchical chain. As care is made into a commodity, women with greater resources in the global economy can afford the best quality care for their families. Conversely, the care given to those with fewer resources is usually worth less.

Consequently, the quality of family life progressively declines as care is passed down the international division of care work. Freed of household constraints, those on top can earn more and consequently afford better quality care than the domestic workers whom they hire. With their wages relatively low, these domestic workers cannot afford to provide the same kind of care for their family. They in turn leave them behind in the Philippines to be cared for by even lower paid domestic workers. Relegated to the bottom of the three-tier hierarchy of care work, domestic workers left in the Third World have far fewer material resources to ensure the quality care of their own family.

The international division of care work implies that a care inequality defines the relationship of women in the global economy. Moreover, the passing down of care responsibilities between women shows that care still falls largely on women and not men's shoulders. Equally significant, it also indicates that public accountability for care remains slim. I make these points by looking at the case of various receiving nations that employ migrant domestic workers.

3. The traditional household division of labour

In the industrialized countries of Asia, the Americas and Europe, the number of gainfully employed women has climbed dramatically in the last forty years. For instance, in France, an additional two million women entered the labour force between 1979 and 1993, a 21% increase in the number of working women.[8] In Italy, the downward trend in the labour force participation of women from 1959 to 1972 has also taken a reverse direction.[9] In fact, Italy has witnessed an increasing number of married women in the labour force, but surprisingly a decline in the number of younger single women engaged in paid work.[10] In the United States, women represented 46.5 % of gainfully employed workers in 1992, a considerable increase over 32.1 % in 1960.[11] Additionally, mothers are more likely to work. For instance, in the United States, three out of four mothers with school-age children are in the paid labour force, the majority of whom work full time.[12] Similarly in Italy and Spain, women tend to keep their full-time jobs even when they have young children at home.[13]

Yet, the increase in women's share of labour market participation has not led to drastic changes in the traditional household division of labour. Although more fitting of households with a stay-at-home mother and bread-winner father, the work of care – feeding, cleaning, dressing, and watching over young children – is still performed by women much more so than men.[14] According to Arlie Hochschild, in these times of a 'stalled revolution', at least in the United States, the vast majority of men do less house-work than their gainfully employed partners.[15] A significant number of women have to cope with the double day, or 'second shift', because women still perform a disproportionate amount of housework, childcare, and social relations with kin and community. Similarly in Italy, eliminating *doppio lavoro* (literally meaning double work) has been a recurring agenda in the Italian feminist movement since the early 1970s.[16]

The burden of the double day not only indicates that gender inequalities hamper the family life of women. It also shows that welfare support for the family does not consistently reflect changes brought by the entrance of women, particularly mothers, to the paid labour force. Welfare support in many countries does not address the new demands brought by the increase in women's labour market transformations to the family.[17] This is the case in the United States, as well as various nations in Western Europe. The United States has the least welfare provisions among rich nations in the global econ-omy as families are without access to universal health care, paid maternity and parental leave, government-provided childcare, or family caregiving allowances.[18] The absence of a sense of communal responsibility for care in the United States is for instance reflected in the care of the elderly. Studies have shown that family members, usually women, provide approximately 80 to 90 % of their care without any formal assistance from the government.[19]

Although providing more benefits than that in the United States, the welfare regimes in various European countries also follow a conservative model of the family. The comprehensive publicly-funded preschool system in France stabilizes the family life of dual wage earning couples, but femi-nists have argued that the 'strongly entrenched division of labour within the household' still hurts women.[20] This is for instance shown by the burden of elderly care falling mainly on women in the family, as it is not supported with residential care provisions. Other countries such as Greece, Italy and Spain have relatively low welfare provisions.[21] In contrast, the socially democratic Scandinavian nations provide the most gender-sensitive public benefits for families. Sweden for instance promotes gender equality by pro-viding gender-neutral parental leave and universal entitlements in the form of allowances, subsidies, and direct services for the elderly and single parent households.[22]

4. A family welfare system

Social patterns of welfare provisions influence the direction of the migratory flows of foreign domestic workers. Notably, nations with very low welfare provisions, i.e. nations that keep the care of the family a private responsibility, particularly the United States and southern European nations such as Spain, Greece, and Italy, have the highest rate of foreign domestic workers. In contrast, countries with social democratic regimes such as Scandinavia, where the benefit system abides by universalism and provides large-scale institutional support for mothers and families, are less likely to rely on foreign domestic workers.

Thus, it seems that the lesser public accountability there is for the family the greater the need for the labour of foreign domestic workers. This suggests that the implementation of a public family welfare system would lead to greater recognition of the high worth of the care of the family and the lesser burden of the double day for women in the labour force. It would also mean a lesser need to devalue, i.e., commodify into low-paid labour, the caring work required of the family. According to Martin Conroy, public family welfare systems provide 'a network of supportive state and community institutions to families, such as long postpartum family leaves, accessible high-quality day care, good public schools and after-school care for primary-school children, and good local public transportation . . . All this provides a "public family" that is able to socially integrate children as an extension of a transformed "private family".'[23]

Without the benefit of a 'public family' system, many overwhelmed working women in various Western countries have had few choices but instead rely on the commodification and consequent economic devaluation of care work. To ease the double day, they have turned to day-care centres and family day-care providers, nursing homes, after-school baby-sitters, and also privately hired domestic workers. As Joy Manlapit, an elderly care provider in Los Angeles observes:

Domestics here are able to make a living from the elderly that families abandon. When they are older, the families do not want to take care of them. Some put them in convalescent homes, some put them in retirement homes, and some hire private domestic workers.[24]

Without doubt, women in industrialized countries have come to take advantage of their greater economic resources than women from developing countries: they do this by unloading the caregiving responsibilities of their families to these other women. As my discussion shows, those who receive less gender-sensitive welfare provisions from the state do so much more than others. And those who are able to negotiate with their male counterparts in the family for a fairer gendered division of labour are equally less likely to do so. This indicates that greater state and male accountability for care would likely lead to not so much a lesser need for domestic workers but greater recognition of the worth of domestic labour.

II. The partial citizenship of migrant domestic workers

The state incorporation of migrant domestic workers reflects the devalued view of private domestic work in host societies. However, migrant domestic work spurs economic growth. Patricia Licuanan, in reference to households in Hong Kong and Singapore, explains:

> Households are said to have benefited greatly by the import of domestic workers. Family income has increased because the wife and other women members of working age are freed from domestic chores and are able to join the labour force. This higher income would normally result in the enlargement of the consumer market and greater demand on production and consequently a growth in the economy.[25]

1. The problem of limited incorporation

Despite their economic contributions, migrant domestic workers suffer from their limited incorporation as partial citizens of various receiving nations. By this I mean they face restrictive measures that stunt their political, civil, and social incorporation into host societies. From an economic standpoint, this is not surprising. Receiving nations curb the integration of migrants so as to guarantee their economies a secure source of cheap labour. By containing the costs of reproduction in sending countries, wages of migrant workers can be kept to a minimum; i.e., migrants do not have the burden of having to afford the greater costs of reproducing their families in host societies. Moreover, by restricting the incorporation of migrants, receiving nations can secure their economies a supply of low-wage workers who could easily be repatriated if the economy is low.

As such, migrants are usually relegated to the status of temporary settlers whose stay is limited to the duration of their labour contracts. Often, they cannot sponsor the migration of their families, including their own children. This is the case in Middle Eastern and Asian receiving nations, which are much more stringent than other countries. For example, in Taiwan, state policies deny entry to the spouses and children of the migrant worker.[26] Singapore even prohibits the marriage or cohabitation of migrant workers with native citizens.[27] Accounting for the nuances engendered by differences in government policies, the restriction of family migration comes in different degrees and levels of exclusion. Temporary residents in Italy have been eligible for family reunification since 1990. Likewise in France and Germany, dependents of migrants were granted the right to work in the 1980s.

However, family reunification remains a challenge to many immigrants in Europe. Despite the more inclusive policies for migrants in Europe than in Asia, European nation states nonetheless still restrict migrants to the status of 'guest workers'. With heightened anti-immigrant sentiments in European nations such as Italy, the basis of citizenship is unlikely to become more inclusive and allow permanent settlement for this racially distinct group. As a result, most migrant Filipina workers prefer not to petition for the children whom they have left behind in the Philippines.[28] In France, they are for instance discouraged by the increase in years of residence to qualify for family reunion as well as the decrease in the age for eligibility as a dependent from 21 to 18 years old.[29] In Germany, children under 16 years old are required to obtain a visa to visit their legally resident parents. In the United Kingdom, entry conditions for family visits have become stricter with the rising suspicion of the intent of family members to remain indefinitely.[30]

Labour conditions in domestic work also hamper the ability of migrants to reunify their family. Contracts of 'guest workers' usually bind them to stay with their sponsoring employer, which again makes them incredibly vulnerable to less than par labour standards. This is especially true of domestic workers because their isolation in private homes aggravates the vulnerability engendered by their legal dependency on their sponsoring employers. For instance, domestic workers in Hong Kong who flee abusive employers automatically face deportation proceedings due to the stringent legislation imposed for foreign domestic workers in 1987.[31]

2. *Full citizenship*

Eligibility for full citizenship is available in a few receiving nations including Spain, Canada, and the United States. In Spain and Canada, migrant Filipinas are eligible for full citizenship after two years of legal settlement. Despite the seemingly more liberal and inclusive policies in these nations, political and social inequalities, as Abigail Bakan and Daiva Stasiulis have pointed out using the case of migrant Filipina domestic workers in Canada,[32] still mar the full incorporation of migrant workers. In Canada, the Live-in Caregivers Programme requires an initial two years of live-in service before foreign domestics can become eligible for landed immigrant status. At this time, it restricts these workers to the status of temporary visitors, denies the migration of family, and leaves them prone to face abusive working conditions. Without the protection of labour laws granted to native workers, migrant domestic workers in Canada – the majority of whom are Filipinas – have fewer rights than full citizens. Filipina domestic workers in the United States likewise experience the same vulnerability. Obtaining a green card through employer sponsorship has been described as a form of state-sanctioned indenture-like exploitationbecause the worker is obligated to stay in the sponsored position until the green card is granted (usually two or more years) During this time, migrant workers are prone to abuse and sub-standard working conditions.

Without doubt, the imposition of partial citizenship on migrant domestic workers benefits employers. The guest worker status, legal dependency on the 'native' employer, ineligibility for family reunification, and the labour market segmentation of foreign women to domestic work guarantee host societies a source of secure and affordable pool of care workers at the same time that they maximize the labour provided by these workers and constrain their ability to care for their own family, particularly their own children. This works to the benefit of the employing family, since migrant care workers can give the best possible care when they are free of caregiving responsibilities to their own families. Yet, the experience of partial citizenship for migrant domestic workers points to a central irony in globalization. Migrant domestic workers care for rich families in the North as they are imposed with social, economic, and legal restrictions that deny them the right to nurture their own families. The elimination of these restrictive measures would at the very least grant foreign domestic workers the basic human right of caring for their own family.

Conclusion

This article looks at the unequal relationship between migrant domestic workers and their employers. It points to the paradoxical position of women regarding family care work. While women from the North view the care work for the family as a burden to be passed on to poorer women from the South, this latter group of women see it as a human right denied to them by restrictive migration policies in various host societies of the North. However, the division of care labour between women does not completely work to the advantage of the employing women in the North. Though freed of the care work for the family, they are still plagued by the structural gender inequalities that relieve men and the state of responsibility for care. Imposing sub par labour conditions on migrant domestic workers only maintains and avoids the root causes of these inequalities. This is not to say that society should ban the employment of migrant domestic workers. Instead, employing families should develop a greater sense of accountability to migrant domestic workers and their families. They can do this by advocating for the elimination of policies that restrict family migration and more generally limit the citizenship rights of migrant workers. Not doing so would maintain the gender inequalities that plague working women and promote the maintenance of the international division of care work, the relegation of care work to women, the lack of public accountability for this work, and finally the devaluation of this labour. Addressing the human rights concerns of migrant domestic workers could only benefit the larger population of women in our globalized society.

Notes

The article benefits from the support provided by the Ford Foundation Postdoctoral Fellowship Program (2001–2000) as well as the sound advice shared by Arturo Tajanlangit, Jr.

1. See Noeleen Heyzer, Geertje Lycklama á Nijeholt and Nedra Weekaroon (eds), *The Trade in Domestic Workers: Causes, Mechanisms, and Consequences of International Labour Migration*, London: Zed Books 1994; Abigail Bakan and Daiva Stasiulis (eds), *Not One of the Family: Foreign Domestic Workers in Canada*, Toronto: University of Toronto Press 1997; Pierrette Hondagneu-Sotelo, *Doméstica*, Berkeley: University of California Press 2001.
2. Rhacel Salazar Parreñas, *Servants of Globalization: Women, Migration and Domestic Work*, Stanford, CA: Stanford University Press 2001.
3. Martin Conroy, *Sustaining the New Economy: Work, Family, and Community in*

the Information Age, New York: Russell Sage Foundation Press and Cambridge, MA: Harvard University Press 2000.

4. Parreñas, *Servants of Globalization* (n.2).
5. Excerpt is drawn from Parreñas, *Servants of Globalization* (n.2).
6. Migrant domestic workers usually belong in a higher-class stratum than do domestics left in the Philippines. Often professionals in the Philippines, they use their resources to afford the option of seeking the higher wages offered in more developed nations.
7. Barbara Katz Rothman, *Recreating Motherhood: Ideology and Technology in a Patriarchal Society*, New York and London: W. W. Norton 1989, p.43.
8. Conroy, *Sustaining the New Economy* (n.3), p.138.
9. Donald Meyer, *The Rise of Women in America, Russia, Sweden, and Italy*, Middletown, CT: Wesleyan University Press 1987.
10. V. A. Goddard, *Gender, Family, and Work in Naples*, Oxford and Washington, DC: Berg 1996.
11. Parreñas, *Servants of Globalization* (n.2).
12. Scott Coltrane and Justin Galt, 'The History of Men's Caring', in *Care Work: Gender, Labour and the Welfare State* ed. Madonna Harrington Meyer, New York and London: Routledge 2000, p.29.
13. Conroy, *Sustaining the New Economy* (n.3), p.137.
14. Coltrane and Galt 'The History of Men's Caring' (n.12).
15. Arlie Hochschild (with Anne Machung), *The Second Shift*, New York: Avon 1989.
16. Lucia Chiavola Birnbaum, *Liberazione della Donne*, Middletown, CT: Wesleyan University Press 1986.
17. By welfare support, I refer to the government's accountability for the social and material well- being of their citizenry.
18. Francesca Cancian and Stacey Oliker, *Caring and Gender*, Thousand Oaks, CA: Pine Forge Press 2000, p.116.
19. Jennifer Mellor, 'Filling in the Gaps in Long Term Care Insurance', in *Care Work: Gender, Labour and the Welfare State* ed. Madonna Harrington Meyer, New York and London: Routledge 2000, p.206.
20. Eleonore Kofman, Annie Phizacklea, Parvati Raghuram and Rosemary Sales, *Gender and International Migration in Europe: Employment, Welfare and Politics*, New York and London: Routledge 2000, p.143.
21. Ibid.
22. Cancian and Oliker, *Caring and Gender* (n.18), p.18.
23. Conroy, *Sustaining the New Economy* (n.3), p.125.
24. Excerpt drawn from Parreñas, *Servants of Globalization* (n.2).
25. Patricia Licuanan, 'The Socio-economic Impact of Domestic Worker Migration: Individual, Family, Community Country', in Noeleen Heyzer, Geertje Lycklama á Nijeholt and Nedra Weekaroon (eds), *The Trade in Domestic*

Workers: Causes, Mechanisms, and Consequences of International Labour Migration, London: Zed Books 1994, p.109.

26. Pei-Chia Lan, 'Bounded Commodity in a Global Market: Migrant Workers in Taiwan', paper presented at the 1999 Annual Meeting of the Society for the Study of Social Problems, Chicago, 6–8 August.
27. Bakan and Stasiulis, *Not One of the Family* (n.1).
28. See ch. 4 in Parreñas, *Servants of Globalization* (n.2).
29. Kofman et al. *Gender and International Migration in Europe: Employment, Welfare and Politics* (n.20), p.68.
30. Ibid.
31. Nicole Constable, *Maid to Order in Hong Kong: Stories of Filipina Workers*, Ithaca, NY and London: Cornell University Press 1997.
32. Bakan and Stasiulis, *Not One of the Family* (n.1).

Feminist Struggles for Women's Rights: Towards a New Global Agenda

VIRGINIA VARGAS

Introduction: occupying global space

The dramatic changes we have been experiencing in the last quarter of a century have led Norbert Lechner (1999) to state that we are facing not an epoch of changes but a change of epoch. Globalization, which is the basis and motor of these changes, is an ambivalent and contradictory process that has generated great risks, new dynamics of inclusion-exclusion and a new ground – the planet – on which to build new rights. The possibility of a global citizenship and the development of global civil societies are inscribed in the dynamic processes opened up by these changes. We are witnessing the formation of a tendency that has begun to spread significantly in the last few decades, the basis of which is the incursion of a multiplicity of movements into the global arena. The incursions of feminist movements in these processes, with their struggles revolving around human and citizenship rights for women, have had a fundamental presence and purpose thanks to the fact they they are driving what many writers have called 'globalization from below' (most recently, Brecher et al.). Inspired by social movements, crossing national boundaries, identities, and interests and unfolding on several levels, this globalization 'from below' is confronting global powers and producing a complementary collective and multiple empowerment.

Peter Waterman situates this dynamic clearly when he says that globalization is both threat and promise. I am not going to deal with the complex dimensions of these ambiguities here, as they have been extensively studied by others. My contribution here is concerned with setting out and examining a critical analysis of certain forces accompanying globalization, which pave the way for the production of new identities, thereby generating new possibilities for nourishing the processes of globalization from below. One of these forces is the process of de-traditionalization – as Anthony Giddens calls it – which works to weaken archaic customs and traditional received ideas, including those on relationships between the sexes (towards a tangible and flexible sexuality) and accepted family values. This does not imply the disappearance of tradition but rather a change in its status, as it ceases to be something unquestionable and is seen as open to questioning, as, that is, a deliberative area on which we can decide. Equally, this process has led to a fresh perception of politics, of institutional frameworks, and of the circulation of information, stimulating the development of an increasingly reflective understanding ('institutional reflectivity', Giddens calls it) that no longer places politics just in the formal spaces, or sees its legitimacy deriving from the vote or representation, but sees it expanding into increasingly important spaces for all citizens: daily life on the one hand, globalized systems on the other. The expression of this dynamic in plural and multiplying processes allows people to become subjects of rights and obligations. It also undoubtedly redefines identities. The most notable case, according to the recent report by the United Nations Development Programme, is the redefinition of traditional gender identity that has come about.

The depth of these changes has also affected nation states, which appear ever smaller in confrontation with major global problems and ever larger as they take in a growing plurality of ways of living, of people's daily needs, of new rights, of the acceptance and redistribution that new identities incessantly demand. Changes in traditional accepted ideas, in ways of questioning the situation, in political perceptions, in the dynamics of the nation state, and a pervading uncertainty forcing people to seek new ways of interpreting and responding to these changes are the foundation upholding and developing the dynamics of forming people into a global citizenry.

The actors on this global stage are many; they perform from many wings and propose varied strategies. Nevertheless, they are more than actors occupying the global theatre. By bursting all at once into this space, they generate unknown dynamics and processes full of democratic possibilities and indications. Of these, I think it vital to consider the growing depth of concepts of 'the citizenry' emerging from 'disputes' between civil societies and states. This dispute makes the citizenry a mobilizing force in the face of global dynamic of exclusion affecting societies, states, and powers.

I. Women's stimuli and possibilities

A global citizenry, just like a national one, is formed and broadened by forces arising from below, as a result of the collective pressure applied by social movements, which stimulate development and enshrining of new rights through their process of discovering and exercising them. The same also happens from above, both on the national level as nation states adopt modernizing proposals, and on the global level in the initiatives handed down through international bodies, through the recommendations of conferences and summits, and through the still nascent global consensus.

1. The right to have rights

The process of discovering and exercising rights before they are recognized and enshrined brings us to another basic characteristic of citizenry: the existence in its members of not only an objective dimension, which echoes back currently existing rights, but also of a subjective dimension, which alludes to the citizenry's perception of themselves as subjects who do or do not deserve rights. On the global stage, the subjective dimension of the citizenry is a basic impulse for the implementation and furthering, since appropriation of the idea of the right to have rights lies at the base of the form in which global rights are beginning to be expressed and demanded. This subjective recognition of the right to have rights also expresses a fundamental driving force of a citizenry: making explicit the fact that many of the extensions and furthering of these rights are fought for and obtained through pressures coming from below once they have begun to be discovered and exercised in practice – in other words, once they have in some way already become part of the subjective outlook of significant sectors of the citizenry as it exists in fact.

This means that pressures from above and below also correspond to the two sources of nourishment and construction of a global citizenry and global civil societies: that represented by official transnational bodies, on the political level, and that fed by social movements with a global perspective. Both sides run parallel but with permanent points at which they intersect, coincide, and clash, not only because they obey different logics and dynamics of operation but also because of the separate viewpoints and interests from which they start.

There are several dynamics that flow together into the official transnational bodies source, many of them fed by the United Nations Organization system, which, despite its growing limitations, has taken initiatives and developed a certain degree of institutional consensus in relation to nation states, often more morally than effectively. On one side there is the tendency to recover the 'universal' meaning of human rights, seeking international mechanisms for defending the rights of the most excluded groups (indigenous peoples, women, children, and so on) through the International Conventions of the United Nations. On the other there has been the holding of a series of world summits and conferences during the 1990s, which have placed some of the 'global as the globe' (in the words of Boaventura de Sousa Santos) subject matters on the table. Each of these has produced documents or Action Plans containing recommendations to which the majority of governments have subscribed and which they are committed to put into effect. And each of them has also generated an amalgam of movements and initiatives tending to influence their contents and then to guarantee the implementation of the commitments entered into by the governments.

For women, these initiatives have been essential in making their presence and contribution visible, an assertion proved true by several conferences. The Conference on Human Rights held in Vienna in 1993 recognized, for the first time, women's rights as human rights; the 1994 Conference of Population, also held in Vienna, recognized reproductive and sexual rights; the World Conference on Women held in Beijing in 1995 – disputed territory *par excellence* owing to its size and diversity – produced an Action Plan that proved a major tool for applying pressure on governments, which are generally reactionary in regard to women's rights. The variety of movements – ecological, human rights, feminist, ethnic, health-care, developmental, and the like – that have interacted actively and often conflictively with governments have been key to the results achieved by these conferences. Equally, matters as global as the globe itself could not have become so, in people's consciousness, without starting from the active struggle of social movements on a global scale. The high profile of the dangers facing the planet was produced very largely through the audacious struggles of Greenpeace and other similar movements. The struggle of the Landless Workers' Movement in Brazil and consciousness of the dangers threatening Amazonia would perhaps not have been possible without the campaign waged by Chico Mendez, which was followed worldwide as it developed, with all its dramatic twists and consequences. The World Women's March of 2000, extended to the whole globe, brought together thousands of democratic and feminist volunteers to demonstrate the pernicious effects of free-market policies on women's lives.

2. An international consensus

In this way, human rights, the basis and often the expression of citizens'
rights, have come to be one of the most significant hubs of this aspect of
global civil society. It is around these rights that a new set of global institutions has been coming into being, enabling complementary use to be made of
international human rights legislation in the field where violations are not
subject to national sanctions, either because governments refuse to prosecute or because their nature is to operate beyond national boundaries:
torture, refugees, forced prostitution, violence against women are some of
the problems that have been the subject of international conventions and
agreements. This international consensus has a double orientation: on one
side, it defends citizens against the arbitrary use of force by nation states; on
the other it gives citizens a court of appeal for what states delay in granting
them or simply refuse to grant, both in the sphere of public affairs and in that
of supposedly 'private' matters with a high political charge. The arrest of
General Pinochet and the effect it had not only on the global but also on the
national stage, helping to bring down a hollow and conniving democracy, is
perhaps the best example of the potential offered by a global consensus and
the deep interrelationships between global and local.

   This means that appropriating and broadening this new framework is a
right and a responsibility for social movements of an international nature in
general, and for feminist movements in particular. The new regional and
global framework provides a real possibility for achieving justice from a
global standpoint. This is the case, for example, with the 'Convention for
Preventing, Punishing, and Eradicating Violence against Women', better
known as the 'Belem do Pará Convention', of 1994, which has enabled the
women of the region to find support and apply pressure on governments that
make use of or allow violence – domestic, sexual, cultural, or political –
against women. It is also true of the 'First International Seminary on
Women's Reproductive and Sexual Rights', held in São Paulo in 2001,
inspired by Latin American feminist movements. It will also apply to the
'Convention of Sexual Rights' now being planned by these same movements.

3. Networks and relationships

In this process of struggle for the extension of recognitions and rights on the
global level, a rich web of networks and relationships is continually being
woven. This provides already internationalized concerns with a continual

flux of impacting actions and exchanges that continue debating the meanings and profiling the contents of global agendas. The social and feminist movements active on the global scene have already begun to bring forward specific projects and agendas related to entrenched discriminations – gender, ethnic, sexual orientation – and to increasingly global problems. These movements devise both defensive and proactive strategies, both in negotiating with and applying pressure on states at a global level and in negotiations and alliances among various protagonists and movements, dealing with a huge variety of personal concerns as well as with multi-cultural and pluri-ethnic interests.

At this early and uncertain stage, when *objective* global rights are being worked out, the concept of citizenship carries a significant weight. The development of global citizenship would be nourished by the possibility of imagining a future in which everyone has a future (Falk). The global scene therefore has a potential double virtue where citizenship is restricted: it can make its image and proposals visible; at the same time it can reflect or inform the true legitimacy of recognition of 'others', a legitimacy not easily found in their countries of origin. The existence of networks of solidarity, of acquaintanceship, of learning, together with theoretical, political, and personal exchanges, also provides a stimulus for furthering subjective citizenship. This happened, for example, with indigenous women in the Beijing process: their concept of citizenship was changed and developed in the light of the legitimating interactions and disclosures openly available on the global level but generally accorded only grudgingly in their own countries, by both governments and society as a whole.

II. The limitations

1. Ambivalent effects of globalization

Despite the enormous stimuli and possibilities afforded by globalization, its limitations are still also great. Obviously, global citizenship and the dynamics of global civil societies cannot be detached from the dynamics of power or from the power structures obtaining in and among countries on a global level. This is so, as the present context shows, because persons are not equally empowered within their collective groups, nor are states in relation to one another. The forms global citizenship could take are related to the forms in which persons and collective groups are inserted into global frameworks, and to the forms in which national exclusions and subordinations are seen to be expressed on the global scene. The ambivalent effects of globalization, at once exclusive and integrating, also modify, stimulate, or renew these dynamics of inclusion/exclusion. Even it is true that diversity appears to be more marked and more visible on the global scene, it is still laden with inequality and otherness and therefore remains rather an aspiration to be realized, as part of the disputed territory that includes citizenship extended to a global level.

2. *Hegemonic powers*

On the subject of citizenship, we must bear in mind that social democratic movements are not the only players on the world stage. Far from making ingenuous assumptions, we have to recognize that this stage is, in itself, far from democratic. The global arena is also plagued with conservatism, fundamentalism, hegemonic and subordinate powers. The same forces that give rise to authoritarianism, exclusions, and closed minds on a local scale also operate actively on the global scale. These forces cover not only enormous class and income differentials but also the whole gamut of exclusions from and gaps in citizenship represented by women, ethnic groups, young people, homosexuals, and all groups affected by power relationships in symbolic, political, and cultural spheres, which are also expressed at global level. Incursions into the global sphere, for this reason, involve those specific movements, groups, and individuals whose access to international arenas is much greater than that of the majority of people in their various countries and regions. Even though initiatives and networks from all over the planet come together in the international arena, multi-cultural and pluri-ethnic presences have begun to be visible and active; what cannot always be guaranteed, though, is that the full diversity of class, gender, and ethnicity from all the different regions will be ensured participation.

3. *New mechanisms*

In the sphere of global institutional consensus, a potentially essential tool for defending, recovering, and achieving new rights, there is still much to be accomplished. The effectiveness of international action with regard to human rights violations, along with the right the international citizenry has to have accounts rendered by the institutions of global capitalism and the transnationals and multinationals – still not taxable – requires new mechanisms and consensuses. The urgent need for greater democratization and a deep political reform of the United Nations system has been presented in similar terms: 'Fifty years is enough' has been one of the more meaningful campaigns on the global scene, and one in which many feminists took part. Only by applying pressure for incorporating the presence and opinions of civil societies, only by demanding a major financial reform of the very structure of UNO, only with international legal structures that are democratic, institutionalized, consolidated, effective, and accessible to ordinary citizens, and only by honouring the requirement for transnational corporations to act with social responsibility and render accounts to the world's citizens (Giddens), will we be able to further the process of controlling globalization from below.

III. Transforming identities

What has changed in the way identities are constructed and self-perceived? One of the most telling changes has been the blurring of the equation between state-society and identity. In other words, society and the state are no longer organized and experienced in one and the same way, which undoubtedly modifies identities that were formerly thought of in exclusively nationalist terms. National identity has not disappeared, but people's feeling of belonging has been diluted (Lechner 1977). Many other senses of belonging have opened up, modifying citizens' subjective perceptions and concerns. In this process, the changes in people's subjective outlook have been enormous, affecting national identities but also strengthening the growing tendency towards reformulating the identities of movements. This is where I bring in my experience and development as a feminist, as one course of reflection on the orientation of these new identities.

For national and regional Latin American feminist movements, economic, political, and cultural globalization has opened up the possibility of articulating their thoughts specifically in relation to humankind's great themes and challenges (Talpade Mohanty). That is, the strong policy on identities that characterized the beginnings of the feminist movement has undergone a radical change, in that it has emerged from its own self-reference (and from its 'moment' for breaking away, as signalled by Gramsci as basic for developing its own discourse and profile) in order to seek points of engagement with the many other democratic struggles, participated in as much by women as by men, that seek to respond to specific subordinations while maintaining democracy as the shaft linking their struggle to other struggles. This quest derives from actual experience, since this has shown that, for tackling global issues regionally, one's own identities and agendas are necessary but not enough. Here we find, as writers such as Veronica Schild have rightly pointed out, that one of the features of the policy on identities, or on identities focussed on particular themes or concerns, is that oppressed persons can also be oppressors unless they take on board the multiple dimensions of exclusions of women and the varied mechanisms that reinforce exclusions of both men and women. For example, feminist movements – as Leila Gonzáles, a black feminist historian, once reproached me – contained racist discriminations, if not positively at least by omission. Feminist movements can also be cruelly exclusive of young feminists, perhaps not so much through lack of channels for incorporating them into a very varied and diffuse scene as, rather, through as failure to sympathize with the new concerns young women are raising or developing, which are undoubtedly more attuned to the new dynamics of the world into which they have been born.

Bibliography

Frei Betto, '¿Como Fortalecer a Capacidade de Ação das Sociedades Civis e a Construção do Espaço Público?' Intervención en el Panel Eje III: A Afirmação da Sociedade Civil e dos Espaços Públicos, *Foro Social Mundial*, January 2001, Porto Alegre, Brasil.

Jeremy Brecher, Tim Costello, and Brendan Smith, *Globalization from Below. The Power of Solidarity*, Cambridge, MA: South End Press 2000.

Richard Falk, 'The Making of Global Citizenship', in *The Condition of Citizenship (Politics and Culture: A Theory, Culture & Society)* ed. Bart Van Steenbergen, London: Sage Publications 1994.

Anthony Giddens, 'Two Theories of Democratization' in *Beyond Left and Right. The Future of Radical Politics*, Stanford, CA: Stanford University Press 1994.

Norbert Lechner, 'Cultura Política y Gobernabilidad Democrática', *Revista Leviatan*, n.68, Madrid 1997.

Norbert Lechner, 'Las Condiciones Sociopolíticas de la Ciudadanía', *Conferencia de Clausura del IX Curso Interamericano de Elecciones y Democracia*, Instituto Interamericano de Derechos Humanos-CAPEL e Instituto Federal Electoral, November 17–21, México1999.

Veronica Schild, 'New Subjects of Rights? Women's Movements and the Construction of Citizenship in the "New Democracies"', in *Cultures of Politics Politics of Cultures re-visioning Latin American Social Movement* ed Sonia Alvarez, Evelina Dagnino and Arturo Escobar, Boulder, CO: Westview Press 1998.

Boaventura de Sousa Santos, *Toward a New Common Sense: Law, Science and Politics in the Paradigmatic Transition*, New York: Routledge 1995.

Chandra Talpade Mohanty, 'Feminist Encounters: Locating the Politics of Experience', in *Feminism and Politics* ed. Anne Phillips, New York: Oxford University Press 1998.

Virginia Vargas, 'Ciudadanía: Un Debate Feminista en Curso', in *La Ciudadanía a Debate* ed. Eugenia Hola and Ana María Portugal, Ediciones de las Mujeres 25, Santiago, Chile: Isis Internacional 1997.

Peter Waterman, *Globalization, Social Movements and the New Internationalisms*, London: Mansell Publishers 1998.

Catholicism and Women's Rights as Human Rights

MARIA JOSÉ ROSADO-NUNES

I. Catholicism and women's human rights

The concept of 'rights of man' should be understood in the context of modernity's ambition to forge, for the first time in the world's history, a universal consensus.[1] This ideology of rights, charged of paradoxes and limitations, is founded on an Enlightenment concept of 'mankind' and was formed by breaking away from Catholic principles. Charles Curran in a recent book about the social teaching of the church points to the strong opposition of the Catholic Church to the concept of human rights in the nineteenth century. 'Human rights', he says, 'were identified with the Enlightenment in the philosophical realm. Pius IX's *Syllabus of Errors* and Leo XIII's condemnation of modern freedoms illustrate this perspective. The Enlightenment grounded human rights in the freedom and autonomy of the individual person, which Catholicism strongly opposed. The person is not autonomous precisely because human beings are related to God as well as to the world itself . . . Catholic moral theology insisted on duties and not on rights.'[2]

1. From human nature to individual freedom

Under a liberal conception of society, humankind, and the world, 'the rights of man' are based on three suppositions: an extensive, abstract concept of 'humanity'; a concept of rights for which 'humanity' is the only necessary condition; and the realization of the individual as a social unit resulting from these rights. According to Poulat, these suppositions underlying the liberal theory of rights explain the unending and perhaps insurmountable conflict between Catholicism and liberalism, which never ceases to repeat itself. It is possible to consider this conflict in the light of the new problems brought about by bioethics: contraception, abortion, euthanasia and, in broader terms, sexuality.[3]

This conflict between Catholicism and liberalism can be seen in the way law has developed and how the concept of nature has changed. Natural law, the common denominator of Christianity and modernity, has transformed itself in a radical way. 'With modern science, like science itself, modern law repudiates the Christian conception of nature created by scholastic thought, according to Aristotle'.[4] If the basis for Christian ideas is to be found in the affirmation of God as the primary cause and ultimate foundation, scientific thought and modern law are supported by the social contract and by a certain conception of reasoning – which discards appeals to divinity. 'In this effort of scientific and legal construction emerges a new man: the *individual* and his *conscience,* master of himself; his judgments and his decisions'.[5] The 'man' born out of the Protestant Reformation is obliged to obey his conscience alone. 'Without doubt', says Curran, 'natural law fitted very well with nineteenth-century papal opposition to liberalism. Philosophical liberalism so exalted human reason that it denied the divine and cut off human reality from any relationship to God and God's law. Aquinas insisted on the role of human reason but regarded human reason as related to the divine reason through mediation.'[6] According to Christianity, all liberty is a gift from God; it is not inherent in the individual and is not a source of rights. 'To the contrary, all efforts of the modern spirit will tend to abolish this arbitrariness and set it free, offering human nature something which until then depended on a higher order.'[7] Such a transformation, in the legal realm, meant the invention of the individual as a 'social unit and its corollary: one man equals one man'. This principle of individuality not only opposed the Catholic social order, but also the religious order. As such, a conflict of rights developed: 'the right of the individual to freedom of conscience, opinion and religion; the right of Catholicism, held as a state religion, to represent the absolute truth and extract the social consequences which seemed to result . . . Liberal individualism secreted social atheism: a lay society no longer needed God to govern its steps and kept him in the sphere of private life, and in the intimacy of conscience and family.'[8]

Even recognizing a dramatic change in Catholic thought across the 1920s, Curran points to the maintenance of such opposition to the liberal affirmation of individual freedom. 'There is no doubt that a very significant change occurred in the twentieth century as Catholic social teaching came to a greater appreciation of the freedom, dignity, and rights of the individual person. Yet although Catholic social teaching did learn from philosophical liberalism and human experience, it cannot and will not accept liberalism's individualistic's understanding of the human person.'[9]

2. The role of maternity

These discussions may help to shed light on the ways in which the Catholic Church manifests itself by violating the fundamental rights of women. The analysis of this 'unending and insurmountable' conflict between liberal ideas and Christian conceptions may help in understanding the reasons why Catholicism rises up against women's struggles for autonomy.

Feminism sets out to affirm rights and individual liberties by proclaiming that women, as social subjects, are citizens, with the right to interfere in the political sphere of society; and that they, as individuals, have the right to control their own sexuality and reproductive capability. In the field of reproductive rights, 'the issue of individual autonomy – so deeply valued by contemporary feminism – as a fundamental point of the exercise of liberty is the basic inspiration for the growth and adaptation of this field of law'.[10] On the opposite side, Catholicism propagates a traditional conception of women and identifies their essence in maternity. The roles reserved by traditional Catholic doctrine for women are as wives and mothers. As such, the affirmation of individual rights for women becomes incompatible with the staunch affirmations of the Catholic religion. Patrick Snyder, while analysing the position of the present pope, says that '[a]s an absolute, for Pope John Paul II maternity defines in one fell swoop the nature, dignity, vocation, and the temporal and spiritual essence of women'. This pope considers one of the errors of feminism to be exactly the fact that it aims to 'liberate' women . . . from that which is their specific vocation of mother and wife'.[11] Curran affirms that '. . . the male perspective comes through in almost every document of Catholic social teaching. Women tend to be invisible in the earlier documents, except in discussions of the family. Within the family, however, the earlier documents clearly portray and extol the subordinate position of women. Even today the role of women is primarily as mothers and educators of their children in the home.'[12]

Catholic allergy to liberalism reaches modern conceptions of autonomy and the claims of women to their self-determination. These claims are also found within Catholicism itself. The enormous development of a feminist theology has put the basis for a consistent claim of Catholic women for autonomy and for respect of their dignity as human beings, including in the controversial field of sexuality and reproduction. A Catholic theologian,

Monique Dumais, critically states: 'One of the main claims of women is to control their own bodies. How can one feel like a person when that which is closest to one, one's own body, escapes one and is made dependent on others and under the authority of others?'[13]

II. Human rights, feminism, and women's rights

Within the liberal field of supporting individual rights, the notion of human rights has been, and continues to be, critically incorporated and restated by women. As Susan Moller Okin points out: 'The recognition of women's rights as human rights has been taking place on the global stage – from the grassroots to the international conference levels – in the last two decades. This has required considerable rethinking of human rights. Many specific human rights that are crucial to women's well-being need to be identified and acted on to stop clearly gender-related wrongs . . . such rights cannot be recognized as human rights without some significant challenges both to that concept itself and to some institutions basic to the various human cultures, certainly families and religions.'[14]

1. Against the male bias

One of the feminist critiques to the human rights thinking and priorities is their 'male bias'. As stated, the problem is that the 'male model' under existing theories and priorities of human rights prevents the incorporation of women's life experience into the core of the discourse. Problems considered to be private such as rape, domestic violence, claims for sexual freedom, as well as unequal opportunities for education, employment and health care were virtually ignored until women asked for their inclusion at the Vienna and Beijing Conferences (World Conference on Human Rights, held in 1993; Fourth World Conference on Women, held in 1995). Though of great importance for women, these rights were considered to be in the private realm and were off the human rights agenda. As Charlotte Bunch, one of the prime movers to get them on this agenda, has said: 'They have been largely invisible and/or are dismissed as private family, cultural or religious rather than political matters.'[15]

According to Okin some other 'recognized human rights abuses have specifically gender-related forms that were not typically recognized as human rights abuses . . . Also, there was little acknowledgment until recently of women's particular vulnerability to poverty and need for basic social services, such as health care, because of both their biological reproductive capacity and their assumption, in virtually all societies, of greater repsonsability for children.'[16]

2. *Reproductive and social rights*

Southern feminists laid special claim to the incorporation of reproductive and social rights under the notion of women's human rights. 'Reproductive rights are a recent concept arising out of women's own reflection and include individual, collective and social rights, in addition to other rights related to maternity, conception and contraception, family planning, among others which integrate fundamental rights.'[17] Such a widening of rights allows for the possibility that a woman can control her sexuality and reproductive capability as part of the realization of women's citizenship. 'Women's reproductive health must be understood within a wide approach of human development, in order to promote the well-being of people and women's full citzenship . . . The perspective of reproductive rights and health formulated by the network Dawn-Mudar is grounded on the principles of human rights to rescue the question of reproduction from isolation.'[18] According to Irene León, the reformulation of human rights proposed by Latin American women includes economic, social, cultural, civil, and political rights, covering the area of individual rights as collective rights.[19] Calling for the inclusion of social rights and reproductive rights into the scope of human rights, women contribute to the development of the concept of citizenship and democracy, by projecting a new model of society which demands social reform and a change in mental attitudes.[20]

On the other hand, the critical vision of liberalism 'as a political and economic doctrine in which the market is perceived as the driving force of the possibilities of choice, and accumulation and competition are the basic values sustaining it'[21] leads to the suggestion of a Latin American critique perspective on human rights. The document prepared by the Ad Hoc Coordinating Committee of Non-Profit Organizations at the Regional Human Rights Conference held in Costa Rica in 1992 states: 'The application of neo-liberal policies and structural adjustment programs deny economic, social, cultural, civil, and political rights to our peoples since these measures have increased poverty and discrimination by polarizing our societies and leading discriminated groups to subsistence levels; women, Latin Americans of African and Native (South) American heritage, those living with HIV/AIDS, the disabled, those forced to relocate, and migrant workers, have all experienced a decline in their already anguishing situations.'[22]

3. Interdependence

This understanding that relates individual and collective rights instead of opposing them leads to a more comprehensive approach to human rights. While liberal-individualism treats group and individualized interests in competition, feminists offer an understanding of their interdependence. The abstract and atomistic liberal model of the individual leads to undervaluation of or to an ignoring of valued aspects of human experience and makes it difficult to address social needs. Brazilian feminists affirm: 'The action of feminist movements turns to the transformation of gender relations as its historical direction. In this sense, the struggle for women's rights is part of a social transformation process searching for equality, social justice, freedom, etc. The institution of women as political subjects is the core of political action; it is its greatest achievement and at the same time its historical contribution to women's movements in general.'[23]

As many analyses of women's participation at the international meetings of the 1980s and 1990s indicate, this critical feminist assumption of human rights as women's rights has lead to changes in final documents. Activists present at Vienna, Cairo and Beijing have been greatly influential over questions like the conception of family, the adoption of an inclusive language and a historical turn in the understanding of matters of population. Okin shows how matters like religion and family have begun to be affected by the recognition of women as holders of full human rights. The Beijing Platform for Action added to the right to freedom of thought, conscience and religion: 'However, it is acknowledged that any form of extremism may have a negative impact on women and can lead to violence and discrimination.' Even when it is not clear what 'extremism' means, notes Okin,[24] it is significant that religion and family are recognized as not always 'unmitigated goods, at least from the point of view of women seeking equal rights'. Feminists have shown that families considered in a most concrete and less idealized approach are not always a safe place for women. 'Many violations of women's basic human rights both occur *within* (families) and are justified by reference to culture, religion or tradition. So recognizing women's rights as human rights means looking at the institutions of family, religion and culture or tradition in a new light.'[25]

Thus women's reformulation of the liberal concept of human rights so that women's individual rights are integrated into collective rights, and include sexual and reproductive rights as well as the ideal of social justice, challenges the religious concept of human rights. In the case of Catholicism this vision of rights that affirm the importance of individual autonomy, present in a liberal vision but connecting it to social rights, is particularly antagonistic, as we will see.

III. The fundamentalist face of Catholicism in Brazil and women's rights

Can we appropriately talk of fundamentalism when Catholicism is at stake? Commenting on the books of Martin Marty and others on fundamentalism, Ruether points to the fact that they include Catholic and Protestant right-wing groups in the wave of contemporary fundamentalisms. All fundamentalist movements seem to have in common 'a rejection of modernity and efforts to re-establish the public role of religion, if not religious states, to counter what was seen as evil secularity, with its lack of established public values'. However from Ruether's point of view, the authors have overlooked 'perhaps the most striking similarity of all . . . their efforts to re-establish rigid patriarchal control over women and their hostility to women's equality, autonomous agency and the right to control their own sexuality and fertility . . . The Vatican is hardly less obsessed [than other right-wing groups] with women's equality and reproductive rights as the epitome of evil modern secularity and the cause of civilization's demise.'[26]

Howland points to two main characteristics of religious fundamentalism. The first one considers how 'fundamentalists are particularly concerned with women's sexuality – as a danger and a threat to society – and thus are keen to regulate and control women's sexuality and reproduction through a variety of measures . . . and thus a number of norms are aimed at making sure that women's sexuality is controlled – not by women – but by men'. The second characteristic is the tendency of religious fundamentalism 'to take political action aimed at conforming a state's [a country's] law to religious doctrine, particularly in areas affecting women's rights'.[27] The Brazilian Catholic Church is a clear example of this kind of religious fundamentalism.[28]

1. Problems after a good beginning

Unlike the situation in other countries, the relationship of Brazilian feminists with the Catholic Church has not always been one of mutual opposition. In the 1970s, the Catholic Church in Brazil offered an important space for protest against the military dictatorship that existed from the 1960s through the 1980s. During this period, there were feminist and left wing party alliances with the Catholic Church.[29] The firm opposition to the military regime by key members of the Catholic hierarchy and the Church's privileged position in negotiations with the state greatly boosted the institution's credibility in the eyes of the left wing groups with which feminists were allied or to which they belonged. The women's movement was therefore able to find allies in the Catholic Church who supported campaigns for daycare centres, lowering the cost of living, freeing political prisoners, and the like.

Because of the Church's social penetration and its power to influence society, feminist struggles were amplified by this alliance. Through the action of the Ecclesiastic Base Communities (CEBs) in the 1970s, many poor Catholic women from outer urban communities and rural areas took on social and political struggles. According to their testimony in various surveys, it was the Catholic Church that took to the streets. In the process, many of them met with feminists and assimilated their ideas, sharpening their critical awareness in relation to their own situations 'as women' not only in society; but also in the Church itself.[30]

However, the alliance between the Catholic Church and the women's movement at times placed constraints on women's demands and limited the issues debated by the movement. As the military began liberalizing the regime in the 1980s and feminists explicitly extended their demands to include the right of women to decide sexual matters freely, including the right to interrupt unwanted pregnancy, the Church reacted adversely, and conflict entered into the relationship. This ambiguity in the Brazilian Catholic Church towards social issues is maintained by at the same time engaging in social discourse over some issues while siding with the conservative or fundamentalist positions of the Vatican on matters of sexual mores.

2. *Three examples*

A few recent examples may help to illustrate the matter. The first example demonstrates the devotion of certain sectors of the Church to issues of social justice. In 1998, the worst drought in over fifteen years afflicted the north of Brazil. Neither the government nor the media, and not even the president himself, addressed the problem, much less were prepared to do anything about it. Men, women, and children were dying. Finally, the Catholic bishops of Brazil broke the silence and dramatically announced to the starving that they had the right to loot the supermarkets for the food that they needed to live. In fact, the people had already begun this type of action, but the bishops gave their blessing in support. Television, radio, and newspapers then began reporting on the drought and the looting of food. Finally, the president spoke publicly for the first time about the problem. After having announced measures to help the needy population, he called on the courts legally to prosecute 'those' who were encouraging the looting, in a clear reference to the bishops' action. But, it was in fact the Church's outspoken stance that finally provoked a response by the government to the crucial problem of the drought. Many judges and lawyers publicly supported the bishops by stating that stealing food in order to avoid starvation was not a crime and could be justified.

A second example concerns individual rights and social responsibility with respect to human reproduction in cases of rape and pregnancy. In a rural part of the state of Rio de Janeiro, an eleven-year-old girl was raped and became pregnant. She, with the support of her parents, decided to undergo an abortion, which in this case is permitted by Brazilian law. Meanwhile, Catholic religious groups, supported by the local priest, pressured the girl and her family into changing their minds. Thus, the resource of religious argumentation was used to compel a child who had become pregnant by the violence of rape to continue her pregnancy.

Another recent episode is also revealing. Under Brazilian law, women may legally have an abortion for one of two reasons: rape and whenever a woman's life is endangered.[31] But public hospitals do not provide this assistance, so poor women are not protected by this law, and many die. Provoked by continuous political action by the women's movement, legislators proposed a law forcing public hospitals to perform legal abortions. Congress held a special session to discuss the issue. Catholic feminists attended, including myself. A Catholic priest and his supporters also attended. He brought a voting girl with him, making a ridiculous spectacle by presenting her to the entire session and saying, 'this child would not be alive if abortion were legal'.

These cases illustrate the two-sided nature of Brazilian Catholicism, and allow us to evaluate the difficulty faced by Catholic women in continuing to subscribe to this religious creed and, at the same time, to defend their feminist ideas. Their support of the Church's action in the struggle for social justice does not prevent them from criticizing Catholic positions with respect to sexual and reproductive rights.

Courtney Howland, in discussing a possible definition of religious fundamentalism, argues that 'the experience of many religious women who have suffered under fundamentalism and fought to resist it' must be considered. She states that 'fundamentalism is real and has meaning for numbers of religious woman from different religions and countries who experience it as a very real threat to their freedom and often their lives. These women perceive themselves to be religious despite their resistance to fundamentalist trends within their religion, and may perceive themselves to be feminists despite the intensity of their religious belief.'[32]

3. Following the sexual morals of Rome?

In reality, this is the experience of many Catholic women and feminists in Brazil. They swing between affirming their religious faith and the need to defend the more elementary rights of women in search of their autonomy. This is the context in which the fundamentalist face of Brazilian Catholicism should be analysed. Returning to Howland's text, we find a conceptualization of religious fundamentalism that includes, on the one hand, principles of doctrine and, on the other, political action aimed at bringing national legislation in line with religious norms.[33] The doctrine of the Brazilian Catholic Church has always faithfully followed the sexual morals of Rome. The Roman Catholic position on sexuality and reproduction is well known, and has the effect of submitting women to their biological capabilities that allow them to generate new human beings. Women's demands for recognition of their moral capability to make decisions that are acceptable from ethical and religious standpoints, for recognition of their right to decide matters affecting their own lives and bodies, and for recognition of their experiences as appropriate for Christian reflection in the sphere of sexual morals, all produce situations of conflict within the Catholic Church. As Howland and many others bring to light, any change in the patriarchal organization of the family or attempt to enhance women's autonomy in the sphere of sexuality and reproduction threatens the basis of Catholic belief and tradition. [34]

Catholic doctrine pervades Brazilian culture. As has been noted: 'The Catholic patriarchal order is so deeply rooted in our culture that it does not require justification; it imposes itself as self-evident and is considered "natural": Bourdieu points out the great difficulty in analysing this cultural logic due to the fact that the institution for more than a millennium has been woven into social structures and mental thought processes and attitudes, such that analysts run the risk of using certain categories of perception and thought as instruments of knowledge which should rather be dealt with as objects of study.'[35]

In the area of political action, the Catholic Church has a history of constant interference in issues relating to sexuality and reproduction. By making use of the considerable social power that it still enjoys in Brazil, this religious institution acts as a major pressure group by lobbying the government and Congress and by influencing the mass media. In maintaining its traditional principle of the inseparability of sexuality and procreation, its aim is to: 'influence or even define the content of social policy and legislation. The result of this is that dialogue with the representatives of the executive and legislative branches is, in general, continually under the censuring influence of a transcendental and theological order. This situation has resulted in the obstruction of, and delays in, the implementation of social programs, as in the case of the PAISM (Program of Total Assistance for Women's Health), which had its inauguration as an official program delayed because of the Church attempting to remove the IUD (intra-uterine contraceptive device) from the list of contraceptive methods to be offered by the state social services. The controversy finally ended with the inclusion of this method, but meanwhile this has given the religious wing an opportunity to promulgate so-called "natural" methods. In addition, the Church has succeeded in delaying, or even in some cases entirely preventing, the distribution of informative materials produced by feminist groups at the request of the Ministry of Health.'[36]

There are many other examples. The situation over abortion in Brazil is the clearest example of Catholic intervention in the most basic of women's rights: the right to control our own bodies; the right to live our sexuality in a free and responsible way; and the right to decide our own reproductive capacity. In the past few years, the Catholic Church, allied with other religious groups and retrogressive forces of society, has been active in the Brazilian Congress in preventing public access to the voluntary interruption of pregnancy. It has both tried to eliminate the laws that allow for abortion in some circumstances and to prevent further liberalization of the abortion laws. As demonstrated above, the Church also seeks to place obstacles in the way of allowing public health services to provide abortions in situations where the abortion should be legal, thereby effectively preventing poor women from exercising their rights under the law.

The Roman Catholic Church in Brazil, both because of its doctrine in dealing with sexual moral and reproduction and because of its political action in these areas, is one of the most powerful adversaries of the development and affirmation of women's reproductive health and rights. Its opposition to the expansion of the scope of autonomy of thought and action for women is what we characterize as the fundamentalist face of Brazilian Catholicism.

Notes

Texts not originally in English have been translated by the author. An earlier version of this article was published in Courtney Howland, *Religious Fundamentalism and the Human Rights of Women*, New York: St Martin Press 1999.

1. Emile Poulat, *Les Discours sur Les Droits de L'Homme. Ses Paradoxes et ses Contraintes, Extrait: Actes de la IIIéme Rencontre of Man: its Paradoxes and Limits*, Tunis : Centre D'études et Recherches Economiques et Sociales 1986, p.27.
2. Charles E. Curran, *Catholic Social Teaching. A Historical, Theological and Ethical Analysis*, Washington: Georgetown University Press 2002, p.215.
3. Poulat, *Les Discours sur Les Droits de L'Homme* (n.1), p.28.
4. Ibid., p.29.
5. Ibid.
6. Curran, *Catholic Social Teaching* (n.2), p.25.
7. Poulat, *Les Discours sur Les Droits de L'Homme* (n.1), p. 32.
8. Ibid., pp.33–34.
9. Curran, *Catholic Social Teaching* (n.2), p. 221.
10. Maria Betânia Ávila, 'Modernidade e Cidadania Reprodutiva', *Revista Estudos Feministas*, no.1, 1993, pp.382–90.
11. Patrick Snyder, *Le Féminisme Selon Jean-Paul II: Une Négation du Déterminisme Corporel de la Femme* (mimeo), pp.5, 3.
12. Curran, *Catholic Social Teaching* (n.2), p.94.
13. In Snyder, *Le Féminisme Selon Jean-Paul II* (n.11), p.5.
14. Susan Moller Okin, 'Feminism, Women's Humans Rights, and Cultural

Differences', in *Hypatia – A Journal of Feminist Philosophy* , vol.13, no.2, Blomington, Indiana: Indiana University Press 1998, p.32.

15. Quoted in ibid., p. 39.

16. Ibid., p.35

17. Ibid., p. 14.

18. Sia Nowrojec, *População e Direitos Reprodutivos. Perspectivas Feministas do Sul*, tr. Renato Aguiar, Rio de Janeiro: Rede Dawn-Mudar1994, p.13.

19. Irene León, *La Perspectiva Latinoamericana*, Serviço Informativo, Separata, 1 February 1993, p.166.

20. Ávila, 'Modernidade e Cidadania Reprodutiva'(n.10.), p.390.

21. Ibid., p.387.

22. León, *La Perspectiva Latinoamericana* (n.19), p.III .

23. Betânia Ávila and Sonia Corrêa, 'Movimento de Mulheres: Questões para Pensar-se seus Rumos', p.1 in:
    http://www.ibase.org.br/paginas/movimento.htm

24. Okin, 'Feminism, Women's Humans Rights, and Cultural Differences' (n.14), p.41.

25. Ibid, p.39.

26. Rosemary Radford Ruether, 'The War on Women', in *Conscience. A New Journal of Prochoice Catholic Opinion*, vol. XXII, no. 4, Washington, EUA, 2001–2, p.26

27. Courtney Howland (ed.), *Religious Fundamentalisms and the Human Rights of Women*, New York: St Martin's Press 1999, pp.XII, XX.

28. On 19 May 2002, one of the most important Brazilian newspapers reported a confrontation between Catholic bishops and feminists on the ratification of the Convention on the Elimination of All Forms of Discrimination Against Women (CEDAW). While feminists acted in favour of the ratification, Catholic bishops tried to convince the Brazilian parliament to reject the Convention (*O Estado de São Paulo*, 19 May 2002).

29. Leila de Andrade Linhares Barsted, 'Legalização e Descriminalização do Aborto no Brasil; 10 Anos de Luta Feminista', *Revista Estudos Feministas*, no. 0, 1992, pp.104–8.

30. Maria José Fontelas Rosado Nunes, 'De Mulheres, Sexo e Igreja: Uma Pesquisa e Muitas Interrogações', in Albertina O. Costa and Tina Amado (eds.), *Alternativas Escassas: Saúde, Sexualidade e Reprodução na América Latina*, Rio de Janeiro: PRODIR/F.C.C. 1994 (Séries Editora 34), pp. 175, 177–78, 186–94

31. 31 Decreto-Lei n°2848, 7 December 1940, art. 128, Penal Code.

32. Courtney W. Howland, *The Challenge of Religious Fundamentalism to the Liberty and Equality Rights of Women: An Analysis Under the United Nations Charter*, Collum. J. Transnational 1997, pp. 271–80.

33. Ibid., pp. 277–79, 289–96.

34. Geraldine Sharp, 'The Control of Reproduction and Patriarchy in the Church

of Pope John Paul II' and 'The Changing Nature of the Marriage Contract', address to the International Society for the Sociology of Religion, Laval University, Québec, Canadá, June 1995, pp. 289–96.

35. Consuelo Maria Mejía, *Normas y Valores de la Iglesia Catolica en la Sexualidad y la Reproducción: Nuevas Perspectivas*, paper given at Seminário Nacional sobre Políticas Sociales, Sexualidad y Salud Reproductiva, Sala Afonso Reyes, el Colégio de México, 20/21November 1996, p.3.

36. Ávila, 'Modernidade e Cidadania Reprodutiva'(n.10), pp.389–90 .

Feminist Problematization of Rights Language and Universal Conceptualizations of Human Rights

ISABELLE BARKER AND JASBIR KAUR PUAR

Introduction

Since the late 1980s, feminists have brought to bear twentieth-century 'post-foundational' analytical tools of post-structuralism, genealogy, psycho-analysis, and neo-Marxism in their critical assessments of universal rights for feminist projects. The conclusions from these discussions have ranged from the wholesale rejection of universal claims to recent more nuanced reconsiderations of what exactly the relationship between 'universality' and its particulars could and should comprise. These feminist critiques of universal rights have taken place alongside feminist concerns regarding the neo-colonial trappings of rights discourse and practice. Reading both of these critiques in tandem is essential for assessing feminist engagements with human rights.

I. Beween universality and particularity

1. Marker of a patriarchal norm

Feminist resistance to women's claims for universal rights stems from a concern that universality necessarily bears the markers of a parochial Western, patriarchal norm, masquerading as neutral (Scott 1999: 215). From the earliest modern political and theoretical instantiations of human rights, women, slaves, and non-propertied men have been historically excluded from the purportedly universal reach of rights. These exclusions have occurred in concrete terms specific to historical contexts, and so it would seem that these exclusions could be redressed through political reforms over the course of historical progress. For example, though many groups were denied the right to vote at the constitutional founding of most modern liberal states, the franchise has been rendered more inclusive over time. Feminists caution, however, that faith in political reform and historical progress is doomed to offer nothing better than new forms of exclusion.

2. Relationship between the both

Indeed, so the critique goes, feminist efforts to render human rights *truly* universal will falter due to the fact that exclusion of the feminine is discursively written into universality. From a feminist perspective, sexual difference is grafted into this exception – the discourse of universal rights, with its assertion of the autonomous, sovereign rights-endowed subject reflects a distinctively masculine experience (Pateman 1988). Reading this insight through a poststructuralist and Lacanian lens, Renata Slalecl argues that for universality to have any meaning in the first place, it must stand in relation to its 'exception'. Therefore, she explains, 'there has to be someone who does not have rights for the universal notion of rights to exist' (1994: 133).

While such feminist critiques have left many wary of universal human rights claims on behalf of particular identity-based categories, such as women, 'post-foundationalist' scholars are increasingly elaborating the significance of the relationship *between* the universal and the particular (Brown 2000; Butler 1999, 2000; Cornell 1998; Scott 1999; Slalecl 1994; Zerilli 1998). Wendy Brown, for example, has developed a trenchant critique of the claim to women's human rights while considering what conditions must be in place to create alternative conceptualizations of universal rights and particular grievances that do not fall into the same traps. Building on Foucault and Marx, Brown captures the essence of many of the post-foundationalist feminist critiques of women laying claim to universal rights. Brown usefully elucidates the potential pitfalls of women's rights claims, citing specific historical conditions that shape identity-based politics in the post-industrial liberal constitutional state.

3. Legal or political

Brown is concerned that in liberal constitutional regimes women's claims to human rights have taken the form of legal claims rather than political demands, and so have been delimited by the norms of law. And, she argues, this particular deployment of claims to universal rights is rife with shortcomings. Drawing on Marx's critique of civil rights, Brown cites that any claim to purportedly neutral rights (the right to free speech, the right to bear arms, and even the rights to sexual freedom and abortion) is vexed due to the fact that one person's right is exercised at the expense of another's (2000: 232). However, the abstract formalism of rights obscures the fact that the exercise of rights requires this unequal dispensation of rights in practice. In other words, the formalism of abstract rights glosses over concrete relations of domination.

Feminist efforts to counter the abstraction of rights through adjudicating injuries specific to women are similarly troubled. To claim rights on behalf of women, such as the right to abortion or the right to adjudicate sexual harassment, feminists must render the category of woman legible to liberal legal norms. And yet to do so is to subject the identity of woman to regulatory norms. In a Foucauldian vein, Brown is critical of the exclusions attendant with women's rights claims *qua* women. Not only does this identity inscribe a particular injured designation, but it 'enables our further regulation through that designation' – a regulation which proceeds through the various civil and political institutions of the modern state and society (ibid.: 232). Moreover, claiming rights on behalf of 'women' inscribes as the norm the experience of particular women. Thus women's rights claims reproduce a racialized, heteronormative narrative which obscure the complexities of individual women's experiences of subordination.

4. Politics of paradox

Based on these post-foundationalist critiques of universal rights claims, it would seem that feminists are stuck between the proverbial rock and hard place. To accept the terms of abstract universal rights and simply demand inclusion is to perpetuate the a-historicity of formal universalism as articulated within Western liberalism. Relatedly, to iterate and demand protection of rights specific to women is to reify a normative category of woman and to falsely universalize the particular experience of some women. Moreover, invoking rights claims on behalf of women can articulate a particular injury; however, this cannot address the concrete conditions which produce inequality – for that regulatory institutions of state and society are necessary. However, to forego efforts at making any broad rights claims for fear of reproducing false universalisms and invoking regulatory mechanisms is itself a self-defeating political strategy which leaves relations of systematic subordination intact. Brown sums up the paradox of rights defining them as 'simultaneously politically essential and politically regressive' (ibid.: 239).

In assessing this condition of the 'politics of paradox' Brown clarifies the political limitations of human rights. Brown notes that what appears to be a 'self-cancelling' (ibid.: 239) political condition of tenacious paradoxes such as the universal and the particular, the global and the local, the abstract and the concrete, and so on, may in fact only appear mutually exclusive in light of norms of linear historical progress. Indeed, it seems that it is the oddly secular norms of progressive history which render the universal and the particular to appear perpetually at odds, and which in turn demand nothing less than achieving some transformative resolution once and for all. Brown suggests that removing rights discourse from the context of 'progressive historiography' may well result in strategies of 'displacement, confound-ment, and disruption' rather than strategies of 'transformation' (ibid.: 240). These latter strategies remain blinded by a faith that a *true* universal realiza-tion of rights is possible –'true' to the degree that *this* universal will been purified of all the exclusionary logics of universality that we have seen to date. As Linda Zerilli notes, a recent turn aimed at resolution on the side of universality includes an academic 'homecoming narrative' for the 'new uni-versal' which will be truly inclusive this time around (1998: 3). However, the blinded desire for the transformative global realization of universal human rights risks trafficking a cultural norm specific to Western liberalism – in other words, an insistence on giving form to who or what should be endowed with rights, no matter how inclusive, invokes a colonialist narrative of secular salvation (Barker 2002).

II. How undermining universality?

The philosophical debate regarding the universal and the particular takes on political salience in the context of neo-colonial geopolitics. The latest turn towards the 'new universal' includes efforts on the part of feminists to achieve a 'nonconflictual pluralism' in international organizing. Trans-national feminist scholar Inderpal Grewal claims that such frameworks may unwittingly reproduce the universal rather than complicate or undermine it, in so far as they reproduce ideologies of liberal subjecthood while effacing structural inequalities. Arguing for greater attention to the paradox of rights within global relations, Grewal notes that the 'objects of rescue' created by human rights discourses serve to rearticulate geopolitical structural and representational inequalities on a global scale (1998: 50)

1. An ironic dilemma

Articulating similar concerns about representation, Sherene Razack cites cases from Trinidad and Tobago, where Afro-Trinidadian women are less likely to obtain asylum for gender and sexual orientation oppression purposes as opposed to Indo-Trinidadian women who are understood as inherently culturally more 'oppressed', demonstrating a reliance on narratives of victimization and assumptions of Indian culture which underpin the gender asylum process in Canada. Razack argues that such cases and others that fall within human rights legislation are most likely to succeed when women are able to present themselves as victims of dysfunctional, unusually patriarchal cultures and nations, and that such mechanisms are like 'fighting sexism with racism'. Further complicating the issue of representation with a comment about positionality and privilege, in her description of the 'hallmark of UN-style feminist universalism', Gayatri Spivak queries the inherent constitution of ' "woman" as object-beneficiary of investigation and "feminist" as subject-participant of investigation' present at the Fourth World's Conference at Beijing in 1995 (1996: 262).

The dilemma is ironic: while often concepts such as 'culture' and religion are used to deny women's human rights – thus suggesting the need to advocate for universal rights (Bunch and Frost 1997) – the history of feminist attentiveness to 'difference' cannot simply be suspended. Given that human rights stem from a Western tradition of secularism – a tradition defined as one which supercedes and is in opposition to religion – this is a particularly interesting problematic (Barker 2002). Within transnational and globalizing circuits, the debates about universality and particularity become navigations between the supposed dichotomies of universalism and cultural relativism, imperialism and self-determination. Stating that feminism itself, particularly global feminism, is often seen to represent Western imperialism, Tracy Higgins notes that 'cultural relativists have accused feminist human rights activists of imposing Western standards on non-Western cultures in much the same way that feminists have criticized states for imposing male-defined norms on women'. She nonetheless argues that 'both the move to expand universal human rights to include those rights central to women's condition and the move toward a relativist view of human rights are consistent with and informed by feminist theory' (1996; see also Cook 1994). The question Grewal, Spivak, and other postcolonial feminists might then pose is, whose feminist theory is Higgins talking about?

Radhika Coomaraswamy, United Nations Special Rapporteur on Violence Against Women, recognizing that she serves 'in some sense as an active instrument of the Enlightenment', asks: 'How does one resolve this dilemma – to remain a critic of the negative aspects of the Enlightenment [namely colonialism] while being a fervent believer in human rights?' Unsurprisingly, Coomaraswamy ultimately argues for 'bottom-line standards', without which 'pluralism in many societies will be achieved at the expense of women and their bodies'. Florence Butegwa supports such a bottom line by adding:

> A look at the Convention on the Elimination of all Forms of Discrimination Against Women may provide a good case study. It is the human rights convention with the most reservations attached . . . What is insightful is that some of the states entered reservations on articles they purport to accept in the context of other human rights instruments. It is, therefore, pertinent to ask whether cultural and religious or other relativism in human rights theory and practice are in the interests of the protection of the human rights of women.

2. Respecting cultural diversity

However Grewal comments that by remaining within the hegemonic apparatus of the state and governing bodies such as the UN, institutions which are already historically representative of Western interests, especially those of the United States, the project of advancing human rights within these systems is quite limited. Discussing the use of human rights instruments in Bangladesh, Shireen Huq echoes Wendy Brown's concern with the limitations of feminist dependence on law, calling for strategies that 'go beyond legal rights, beyond legal reforms, and beyond talking about the law as being responsive to violations of women's human rights' (1995).

Neither Grewal and Isabelle Gunning are willing to abandon rights altogether. Grewal calls for an integration of 'questions of power and self-critique' within human rights praxis (1998: 523), while Isabelle Gunning advocates for dialogue through which 'shared values can become universal and be safeguarded. The process by which these universal standards are created is important. A dialogue, with a tone that respects cultural diversity, is essential.' Gunning remarks that 'this is particularly true with a practice like female genital surgeries, where the governments involved may either refuse to be embarrassed or become angry at the attack on the culture; thus they reject the "interference"' (1991–2). However, other feminists have insisted on the review of the legality of certain Western practices in tandem with the efforts to halt female genital surgeries, from breast reductions and other types of plastic surgeries to braces. Still others have argued that the 'crusade' to save African women is racist and essentializes the practice itself. (see Okin 1994).

3. The agenda of sexual rights

Queer scholars have also queried the extent to which human rights discourses can advance the emerging agenda of 'sexual rights', which generally refer to reproductive technologies, access to health care, and a woman's control over her body. Momin Rahman and Stevi Jackson argue that rights discourses are inherently heterosexist, particularly in the ways that 'campaigns for lesbian and gay rights frequently proceed as if gender and sexual orientation were categories fixed for all time' (1997: 118). This reliance on biological essentialism leave unexamined 'the place of institutionalized heterosexuality in maintaining patriarchal domination' and thus proceeds as an endorsement of 'essentialism and individual rights as a defense against discrimination rather than attacking heterosexuality as a barrier to equality' (ibid.: 117–118). They conclude by stating that 'One possibility for de-privileging heterosexuality within a discourse of rights, is to de-familiarize rights' (ibid.: 177–129).

However, Nicole LaViolette and Sandra Whitworth argue that while 'it is unclear whether joining the very western notions that dominate human rights discourses to often equally western notions of "gay and lesbian" serves a progressive and transformative politics', such processes of adjudication should be seen as the beginning of political changes rather than an end result (see also Dorf and Perez 1995; Wilson 1996; Bunch and Hinojosa 2000). It is a process which tests and measures forms of coalition and community building across national lines, and should be used in conjunction with other strategies. They note, however, that men more so than women are able to prove 'persecution' within traditional legal discourse because their sexual activity is more likely to be criminalized, while the issues faced by lesbians are 'often concerned with invisibility, isolation, and resisting forced marriage'. The authors claim that gay and lesbian activists are most actively dealing with these contradictions, feeling that abandoning rights altogether 'ignore the extent to which rights *do* matter to people who are denied them' (1994: 563–88).

III. Continental binaries

1. Western pressure

In attempting to complicate critiques of human rights discourses that tend, if unintentionally, to reify First World/Third World binaries, scholars note that some strands of relativism may tend to essentialize 'local' culture by conceptualizing them as discrete entities that are static, bounded, and internally monolithic (Higgins 1996; Fox). Commenting on the structural modalities that propel a notion of 'Asian human rights' Yash Ghai writes: 'What conveys an apparent picture of a uniform Asian perspective on human rights is that it is the perspective of a particular group, that of the ruling élites, which gets international attention.' It is this ruling élite that is not only seen as representative of national interests, but is also often in opposition to the interests of feminist and other 'grassroot' organizations (see Mindry 2001.) Diana Fox further argues that the label of 'Western feminism' does injustice to the range of liberal, Marxist, socialist, and radical feminisms often subsumed under such a label.

Furthermore, multiple traditions have articulated some concept of human rights (Coomaraswamy 1997; Butwega 1997). Indeed, the rallying cry 'women's rights are human rights' was first coined by the Philippina group GABRIELA in 1989 (Bunch 1991: 13). On the other hand, 'Western' notions of human rights are also available for subversion, appropriation, and strategic essentialism. Bilhari Kausikan writes that as East Asian states become stronger actors in the world economy, they are less prone to be pressured into conceding to Western human rights doctrines. Citing the linkage between the Clinton administration's attempt to press for human rights in China in exchange for continued most-favoured-nation trading status, Kausikan nevertheless cautions:

. . . Western pressure undeniably plays a role. But in themselves, self-interest and pressure are insufficient and condescendingly ethnocentric western explanations. They do less than justice to the states concerned, most of which have their own traditions in which the rulers have a duty to govern in a way consonant with the human dignity of their subjects, even if there is no clear concept of rights as has evolved in the West (Kausikan 1993)

Despite the general understanding of the development of 'modern' international human rights through the UN and related institutions, Butegwa argues that the 'exact meaning' of human rights 'tends to be hazy, subjective and clouded by political self-interests of the states . . . Human rights is a dynamic concept and this fact has significant implications for women.' As an example, Butegwa argues that in Africa new methodologies for investigating, documenting and reporting human rights abuses of women have been developed to counter normative methods used by groups such as Amnesty International and other traditional human rights groups which tend not to be able to capture the complexity of abuse experience by women (1997). Following Butegwa's logic, it is perhaps precisely the abstract nature of human rights that may be useful for local feminist projects. Joan Scott reflects this thinking in her claim that perhaps, to date, rights have not been abstract enough (1999). By rendering rights more abstract, feminists invoke a tool that they can manipulate to suit particular feminist political purposes.

2. *An organizing tool for women*

Bunch and Frost, among others (Coomaraswamy 1997), argue that despite all of these dilemmas, the human rights framework has been an essential organizing tool for women and has spawned a movement: 'Whether used in political lobbying, in legal cases, in grassroots mobilizations, or in broad-based educational efforts, the idea of women's human rights has been a rallying point for women across many boundaries and has facilitated the creation of collaborative strategies for promoting and protecting the human rights of women' (Bunch and Frost 1997). Butegwa similarly states that accessing the strategies of women's rights movements in other regions has enabled the adaptation of human rights frameworks in Africa (1997). Numerous examples suggest that these adaptations are not without difficult struggles around coalition building across national boundaries, most notably articulated by a recent 'open letter' from the Revolutionary Association of Women in Afghanistan (RAWA) critiquing the Feminist Majority for its persistent erasure and appropriation of RAWA's work (20 April 2002).

The question then arises, do these manoeuvres destabilize or reinforce both the modernist and the neo-colonial framings of human rights discourses? Reading the post-foundationalist philosophical re-configuration of the universal and the particular alongside concerns regarding the colonizing effects of human rights strategies is helpful in assessing whether human rights as a *political* strategy serves to subvert neo-colonialist trappings.

Conclusion: an open-ended project

On the philosophical level, Judith Butler outlines a relationship between the universal and the particular which rests on an open-ended project of cultural translation, rather than insisting on pinning down the real universal once and for all – a strategy which remains hampered by neo-colonialist blinders. Butler's notion of cultural translation recalls Gunning's emphasis on dialogue, while it integrates Grewal's (and others') concerns regarding the neo-colonialist potential in feminist efforts at achieving 'nonconflictual pluralism'. Butler explains:

> There are universal claims intrinsic to these particular movements that need to be articulated in the context of a translative project, but the translation will have to be one in which the terms in question are not simply redescribed by a dominant discourse. For the translation to be in service of the struggle for hegemony, the dominant discourse will have to alter by virtue of admitting the 'foreign' vocabulary into its lexicon (Butler 2000: 168)

Butler remains attentive to the cunning ways of hegemony in the service of dominant ideology, and so insists that cultural translation must remain open-ended so as to remain attentive to preventing yet another set of dominant conventional norms from masquerading as neutral criteria in the service of purportedly universal norms. Towards this egalitarian end, she defines multi-culturalism 'as a politics of translation in the service of adjudicating and composing a movement of competing and overlapping universalisms' (ibid.: 169).

Articulating what Chandra Mohanty terms a 'non-colonized' approach to human rights is an inherently political project, and ultimately recalls Wendy Brown's call for new strategies of displacement, confoundment and disruption, as well as Grewal's interest in self-reflexive human rights praxis. A non-colonized feminist transnational practice will likely involve recognizing, and being open to, the fact that rights may – or may *not* – prove useful in advancing demands for more egalitarian social, economic and political conditions in particular regional, national or local sites. Feminism will best be served by remaining attentive to how best to achieve *this* goal, rather than by, in some missionary zeal, seeking to blanket the globe with a 'truly' universal standard of rights.

Works cited:

AAWORD (The Association of African Women for Research and Development), 'A Statement on Genital Mutilation' in *Third World-Second Sex: Women's Struggles and National Liberation*, New York: St Martins Press 1983.

Isabelle V. Barker, 'Disenchanted Rights: The Persistence of Secularism and Geo-Political Inequalities in Framing Women's Human Rights' manuscript, on file with author, 2002.

Wendy Brown, *States of Injury: Power and Freedom in Late Modernity*, Princeton: Princeton University Press 1995.

Wendy Brown, 'Suffering Rights as Paradoxes,' *Constellations*, 7:2 (2000), pp.230–241.

Wendy Brown, 'Revaluing Critique: A Response to Kenneth Baynes,' *Political Theory* 28:4 (August 2000) 469–479.

Charlotte Bunch, 'Women's Rights as Human Rights: Toward a Re-vision of Human Rights' in *Gender Violence: A Development and Human Rights Issue*, Center for Women's Global Leadership, Rutgers Office of University Publications 1991.

Charlotte Bunch and Samantha Frost, 'Women's Human Rights: An Introduction', http://www.cwgl.rutgers.edu/whr.html, 1997.

Charlotte Bunch and Claudia Hinojosa, *Lesbians Travel the Roads of Feminism Globally*, Center for Women's Global Leadership, 2000.

Florence Butegwa, 'Women Taking Action to Advance Their Human Rights: The Case of Africa', Strategies and Analyses from the ICCL Working Conference on Women's Rights as Human Rights, Dublin, March 1997. Website http://members.tripod.com/~whr1998/documents/icclbutegwa.html

Florence Butegwa, 'International Human Rights Law and Practice: Implications for Women' in *From Basic Needs to Basic Rights: Women's Claim to Human Rights* edited by Margaret Schuler

Judith Butler, *Excitable Speech: A Politics of the Performative*, New York: Routledge, 1996.

Judith Butler, '1999 Preface,' *Gender Trouble*, New York: Routledge 1999 [1990].

Judith Butler and Ernesto Laclau and Slajov Zizek, *Contingency, Hegemony, Universality: Contemporary Dialogues on the Left*, London: Verso 2000.

Rebecca J. Cook, 'Women's International Human Rights Law: The Way Forward', *Human Rights of Women: National and International Perspectives* ed. Rebecca Cook, University of Pennsylvania Press 1994.

Radhika Coomaraswamy, 'Reinventing International Law: Women's rights as Human Rights in the International Community', 1997. Website http://www.law.harvard.edu/programs/HRP/Publications/radhika.html

Drucilla Cornell, 'Troubled Legacies: Human Rights, Imperialism and Women's Freedom' in *At the Heart of Freedom*, Princeton: Princeton University Press 1998.

Julie Dorf and Gloria Careaga Perez, 'Discrimination and the Tolerance of

Difference: International Lesbian Human Rights' in *Women's Rights – Human Rights: International Feminist Perspectives* ed. Julie Peters and Andrea Wolper, New York: Routledge1995.

Diana J. Fox, 'Women's Human Rights in Africa: Beyond the Debate over the Universality or Relativity of Human Rights.' Website http://web.africa.ufl.edu/asq/v2/v2i3a2.html

Inderpal Grewal, 'On the New Global Feminism and the Family of Nations: Dilemmas of Transnational Feminist Practice' in Ella Shohat (ed), *Talking Visions: Multicultural Feminisms in a Transnational Age*, Cambridge: MIT Press 1998.

Isabelle Gunning, 'Arrogant Perception, World Travelling and Multicultural Feminism: The Case of Female Genital Surgeries', *Columbia Human Rights Law Review*, vol. 23, 1991–92.

Tracy E. Higgins, 'Anti-Essentialism, Relativism, and Human Rights', *Harvard Women's Law Journal*, vol. 19, Spring 1996.

Shireen Huq, 'Acting Locally: Bangladeshi Women Organizing as part of the Global Campaign for Women's Human Rights', Strategies and Analyses from the ICCL Working Conference on Women's Rights as Human Rights, Dublin, March 1997. Website http://members.tripod.com/~whr1998/documents/icclhuq.html

Bilhari Kausikan, 'Asia's Different Standard', *Foreign Policy*, vol. 92, 1993.

Nicole LaViolette and Sandra Whitworth, 'No Safe Haven: Sexuality as a Universal Human Right and Gay and Lesbian Activism in International Politics', *Journal of International Studies*, vol.23, no.3 (1994), pp.563–88.

Deborah Mindry, 'Nongovernmental Organizations, "Grassroots" and the Politics of Virtue', *SIGNS: A Journal of Women in Culture and Society*, 26(4), Summer 2001, pp.1187–212.

Susan Moller Okin, *Women in Western Political Thought*, Princeton: Princeton University Press, 1979.

Susan Moller Okin, *Gender Violence and Women's Human Rights in Africa*, Center for Women's Global leadership, Rutgers University 1994.

Carol Pateman, *The Sexual Contract*, Stanford: Stanford University Press 1988.

Sherene Razack, 'The Image of Indian Women in Law: What Gender Persecution Claims Can Tell Us About Indianness', ISER-NCIC Conference, Trinidad 1995.

Momin Rahman and Stevi Jackson, 'Liberty, Equality and Sexuality: Essentialism and the Discourse of Rights', *Journal of Gender Studies*, 6.2 (1997), pp.117–29.

Joan Scott, 'Some More Reflections on Gender and Politics' in *Gender and the Politics of History*, revd edn, New York: Columbia University Press 1999.

Joan Scott, *Only Paradoxes to Offer: French Feminism and the Rights of Man*, Cambridge: Harvard University Press 1996.

Renata Slalecl, *The Spoils of Freedom: Psychoanalysis and Feminism After the Fall of*

Socialism, London: Routledge 1994.

Gayatri Spivak, 'Diasporas Old and New: Women in the Transnational World', *Textual Practice* 10(2), 1996, pp.245–69.

Ara Wilson, 'Lesbian Visibility and Sexual Rights at Beijing', *SIGNS: Journal of Women in Culture and Society*, vol. 22 no. 1, Autumn 1996.

Linda M. G. Zerilli, 'This Universalism Which is Not One'. *Diacritics*, vol. 28, no. 2, Summer 1998.

II. Religious and Theological Structures: Violating or Supporting Women's Rights

Women's Right to Full Citizenship and Decision-Making in the Church

MARGARITA PINTOS DE CEA-NAHARRO

Introduction

The right to citizenship for women in the church has not followed the same course as it has in the social and political spheres. Christianity recognized women's full citizenship from the beginning of the Jesus movement, which was in declared conflict with and open opposition to the androcentric ideology of the Jewish religious world and the patriarchal structures of the Roman empire. This produced a whole revolution with repercussions on the various sectors of society. Women exercised this citizenship in the early Christian communities, but they found themselves being gradually deprived of it as the church ceased to be a house-based community and adopted hierarchical-patriarchal structures following the pattern of the imperial order. Nevertheless, neither the political powers nor the ecclesiastical hierarchy succeeded in removing citizenship from them entirely, as there were always women's movements that exercised it within the bosom of their own communities, sometimes in a manner invisible to the eyes of society of the time, but always in a spirit of assertion.

In the political sphere, women achieved citizenship very late and not without resistance on the part of the patriarchal power. In this respect, the question posed well into modern times by James Mill is worth recalling: 'Why should women have the vote if their husbands already vote?' The universality of human rights proclaimed in modern constitutions and in universal declarations was an abstract universalism from the start, and its inclusive character was more apparent than real, since it left out women, among other groups. Its very formulation in masculine terms is already excluding by its nature: 'All men are, by nature, free and equal.'

I. Women's citizenship in the Jesus movement

Women are fully integrated into the Jesus movement and form part of the discipleship of equals, in which they occupy a central place, not merely a peripheral one. As Schüssler Fiorenza recognizes, their presence and leadership in it have the greatest importance for the practice of solidarity from below, which is the outlook defining Jesus of Nazareth's liberating project. Egalitarian discipleship becomes an ideology critical of androcentric culture and a protest movement against the patriarchal structures of the family and the political and religious context. But citizenship is not confined to the group of followers of Jesus drawn from his Jewish surroundings; it is extended to all women, without distinction of culture, religion or geographical provenance, as shown by the Synoptic account of the Syro-Phoenician woman (Mark 7.24–30; Matt. 15.21–28) and by the story of the Samaritan woman told in John's Gospel (ch. 4).

In the first account, it is a foreign woman who challenges Jesus' exclusive nationalism and invites him to reconsider his cultural prejudices, which included only women from a Jewish background. It is this woman without a name, identified only by her nationality, who argues in favour of the universality of citizenship and makes Jesus himself change his mind.

The second story sets out to overcome the religious conflict with the Samaritans and the taboos concerning speaking to women in public. The Samaritan woman, likewise without a name and identified by her nationality, makes herself and the people of her city part of the messianic movement. The woman's testimony of Jesus to her fellow-citizens makes many of them believe in him: 'Many Samaritans from that city believed in him *because of the woman's testimony*' (John 4.39). Jesus employs a similar expression in John 17.20: 'I ask not only on behalf of these, but also on behalf of those who will believe in me through their word.' John places the woman's testimony and that of the disciples on the same level, and he recognizes the decisive influence of both on the growth of the group of followers.

II. Citizenship in the letter to the Galatians

The experience of full citizenship attained by women in the Jesus movement was continued in early Christianity. This is clearly expressed in the paradigmatic text of Galatians 3.27–28: 'As many of you as were baptized into Christ have clothed yourselves with Christ. There is no longer Jew or Greek, there is no longer slave or free, there is no longer male and female; for all of you are one in Christ Jesus.' This text, a pre-Pauline baptismal formula, shows first that Christian men and women from the uncircumcised pagan world form part of the people of God, abolishing the barriers of nationality. Belonging to the Jewish religion should not be a motive for conceit or a cause of privilege when it comes to belonging to the Christian community, just as not professing Israel's beliefs should be a reason for discrimination.

Another revolutionary contribution made by this declaration is the elimination of differences between slaves and free persons. In the Christian community no one person is master of another; relationships among its members are based on brotherhood-sisterhood. There is no distinction between slave and master in service to the gospel, even though this does not mean that Paul is calling for the end of the regime of slavery: what he is promoting is the elimination of differences of social status within the *ekklesia*.

Third, the text speaks of the disappearance of differences between 'male' and 'female', criticizing social stereotypes based on gender, which lack any scientific basis and are a construct of patriarchy devised to keep its women submissive. Incorporation into the Christian community comes about through baptism, a non-sexed rite of initiation, which includes all those who want to become of Jesus' life project and confers equality of rights and duties on all.

Traditional exegesis of Galatians 3.28c tends to exclude any social and ecclesial reference and refer it solely to the religious sphere. So the equality posited here would be spiritual – all souls are equal – and eschatological – there will be no differences on gender grounds in heaven. Present-day exegesis is less reductionist and stresses the ecclesial and socio-political implications of the declaration, by relating Galatians 3.28 with Genesis 1.27: 'So God created humankind in his image, in the image of God he created them; male and female he created them.'

So, according to Galatians 3.26–28, there is no longer room for divisions based on religious, cultural, or gender motives. Pagans, slaves, and women enjoy freedom and equality. The struggle for freedom, work for justice, solidarity with the poor and oppressed, elimination of discriminations on religious grounds, and liberation from patriarchal structures are inseparable options and commitments that have to taken on as a whole.

III. Women's citizenship in the early Christian communities

In the Pauline communities, women exercise their citizenship through carrying out leadership, prophetic, and teaching functions and through active participation in the Christian communities. Sometimes these functions derive from the social status of some of them – Lydia, in Philippi; Prisca, with her husband Aquila; Nympha in Laodicea; Cloë, possibly, in Corinth. But in general their active participation in the life of the Christian community and their share in decision-making are a direct consequence of the equality conferred by baptism.

It is worth pointing to the existence of women apostles, such as Junia (Rom.16.7), who perhaps led an itinerant life, as the other apostles did. There were women firmly committed to missionary activity – Mary (Rom.16.6); Tryphaena and Tryphosa (Rom.16.12); Euodia and Syntyche (Phil. 4.2–3), who were at the head of many domestic communities and at the forefront of those who proclaimed the gospel. There were also women deacons, such as Phoebe of the church at Cenchreae. Paul commends her to the church at Rome and asks the Christians of that city to welcome her 'as is fitting for the saints' and to work together with her, 'for she has been a benefactor of many and of myself as well' (Rom. 16.2).

The first letter to Timothy speaks of older men and older women (5.1–2) in terms that could be referring to both as presbyters. Some interpret this as meaning that the leadership of the community was composed of men and women presbyters and deacons.[1] Other interpreters, however, believe that the conception of the *ekklesia* in I Timothy would exclude exercise of a leadership role by women.[2]

Women shared in the functions of prayer and prophecy in the community assemblies (see I Cor. 11.5). They may also have taken part in reciting the psalms, in teaching (*didache*), and in speaking in tongues and translating these.

In the domestic churches of early Christianity women enjoyed citizenship, took part in decision-making, and exercised authority. According to Karen Jo Torjesen, the social stereotype of the woman as mistress of her household could have contributed to legitimizing women's exercise of authority.[3] The functions and tasks of domestic authority that were not conditioned by the separation of the sexes were spontaneously transferred to the realm of the domestic Christian community. The authority of women in this realm was seen as something natural. Recognition of women's ability and experience as managers led to their being considered as adequately qualified to carry out leadership, teaching, and administrative roles within the church.

In early Christianity, then, women, excluded by patriarchal society, acquired a status of equality that allowed them to lead groups and liberating and prophetic movements. Charism did not distinguish on grounds of gender but made men and women equal in rights and responsibilities.

IV. Women deacons, presbyters, and bishops in the history of Christianity[4]

When the Christian community changed into a political church integrated into the empire, a campaign was set in motion to remove women from their leadership posts and deprive them of their ecclesial citizenship by alleging that they were transgressing the virtues proper to all women, such as silence, chastity, and obedience, and so that they were shameless. Silence was imposed on them, they were excluded from positions of responsibility, and they were denied the use of the word through which they could develop their thought and formulate their experiences in theological terms. Most women were reduced to a position of subordination, on the grounds that 'man was created first'. Their basic function became the provision of 'subordinate service'. They moved from being *mediators* of divinity and bearers of grace to being *servers* of the only intermediaries between God and the community, who were men.

Despite this, women continued to carry on priestly and sometimes even episcopal ministry in the service of the community and to intervene actively in community decision-making until the thirteenth century. It is true that there are few written testimonies to this leadership by women. This is due to the scarcity of texts written by them and to the markedly androcentric nature of both Christian and pagan sources. 'If women had written the books, I am sure they would have done so in a different way. Because they know that what they are accused of is false.' This was said by Christine of Pizan in her 'Letter to the God Love', written in 1399. We need to turn to archaeological, epigraphic, epistolatory, and other sources.

Beneath the triumphal arch of a Roman basilica there is a mosaic with four female figures. Two of these are the saints Pudentiana and Praxedes, to whom the church is dedicated, and another is Mary. Over the head of the fourth woman, covered with a veil, there is an inscription that reads 'Theodora, *episkopa*'. In a tomb discovered in Tropea (in southern Calabria) in 1876 there is an inscription dating from the mid-fifth century, which refers to 'Leta *Presbytera*' in these terms: 'Consecrated to her good name Leta Presbytera lived forty years, eight months and nine days and her husband built this tomb to her. He preceded her in peace on the eve of the Ides of March.'

Other inscriptions from the sixth and seventh centuries equally attest the existence of women priests: *presbytera, sacerdota* in Salone (Dalmatia); *presbyterisa* in Hippo (North Africa); *presbyteria* near Poitiers (central France); *presbytera* in Greek from Thrace. Catholic historiography tends to discount all inscriptions that make reference to the female priesthood, or to assign the term *presbytera* to the presbyter's wife.

In a treatise on the virtue of virginity, attributed to St Athanasius (fourth century), is the statement that consecrated women could celebrate the breaking of bread together without the presence of a male priest: 'The holy virgins can bless the bread three times with the sign of the cross, pronounce the thanksgiving and pray, since in the kingdom of the heavens there is neither male nor female' (PG 28, 263).

In a letter from Pope Gelasius I (492–96) to the bishops of southern Italy he tells them: 'We have heard to our great distress that divine matters have reached such a low state that women are encouraged to officiate at the holy altars and to share in all the activities of the masculine sex, to which they do not belong.' This document at least proves that women were carrying out priestly functions.

Honorius III, pope from 1216 to 1227, who succeeded Innocent III, wrote to the bishops of Burgos and Valencia to tell them that abbesses were not to speak from the pulpit, since that function was reserved to men. The reason he gave to prohibit them was 'because their lips bear the stigma of Eve, whose words have sealed the destiny of man'.

A priest named Ambrosius asks Athon, Bishop of Vercelli, who lived in the ninth and tenth centuries and was a great authority on ancient conciliar dispositions, what meaning should be given to the terms *presbytera* and *diaconisa* in the old canons. The bishop replies that women also received these ministries *ad adiuventum virorum*, as Paul's Letter to the Romans shows: 'I commend you to *our sister Phoebe, a deacon of the church* at Cenchreae' (16.1). It was the Council of Laodicea, held during the second half of the fourth century, he continues, that forbade the ordination of women to the presbyterate. As for the term *presbytera*, he accepts that in the ancient church this could also refer to the priest's wife, but he prefers the sense of ordained priestess who carried out leadership, teaching, and ritual functions.

These and many other testimonies that could be adduced are rejected by official theology and by the highest ecclesiastical magisterium on the grounds that they lack scientific rigour, when the real reason for their rejection is the patriarchal constructs in which they are embedded. Recognition of the authenticity of these testimonies would cause them to revise their patriarchal constructs and abandon their misogynist positions. And they are not prepared to do that.

V. From 'Vatican incoherence' to full citizenship

At present we Christian women are dispossessed of ecclesial citizenship, while in society we have made major gains in the exercise of civic, political, and social rights. The twenty-first century, the Spanish philosopher Victoria Camps has written, 'will be the century of women. No one is now holding back the movement that formed the revolution of the century now drawing to an end. At the present time, the equality achieved is satisfactory enough, but not completely so. There are still obstacles to an acceptable equality.'[5]

The Catholic Church too now defends women's citizenship, though with many caveats and not a few prohibitions, just as it defends human rights – in society. Nevertheless, it does everything possible to prevent us from practising it inside the Christian community. We are faced with what Bernard Quelquejeu calls 'Vatican incoherence'. What reasons can there be for continuing to deny women full citizenship and access to decision-making powers? Only the obstinacy of the ecclesiastical patriarchy, which remains determined to deny what the New Testament and the history of Christianity justify.

The exegetical, theological, and historical bases for the recovery of this citizenship have already been established. The history of women's emancipation also argues in our favour. Society shows conditions of plausibility that can make the way easier. We can count on the support of feminist theory, providing a method of critical analysis of patriarchal structures in society and in religions, and of women's liberation movements.

In order to achieve our full citizenship in the church and in societies that deny it to us, I propose some key indicators, in full consciousness that they are conditioned by where I write from:

First, our self-affirmation and recognition as *moral subjects*. The role of women has a special relevance in moral discourse within feminist theory. It sets out alternatives to check the dominance of economic and consumerist values, since feminism is first and foremost an ethic. We women are playing a fundamental part in this change, also within the Christian community, in which, as moral subjects, we are guided by the gospel ethic of brotherhood-sisterhood and not by the morality of the patriarchal power. Participation in decision-taking on ethical questions that directly affect our lives and those of other marginalized groups becomes a prime imperative for us. The moment has come for us to move from being simple receivers of and submissive compliers with orders laid down by the patriarchy to intervening in working out new liberating moral teaching.

Second, taking stock of being *theological subjects*. We no longer limit ourselves to doing theology mechanically, re-working the traditional deductive method that starts from truths and results in dogmas; we are re-thinking the faith from our own subjectivity and re-formulating it through hermeneutical and linguistic insights in a gender perspective, so as to work out a true magisterium of women that will incorporate our own teachings and experiences as a fundamental part of the legacy of faith.

Third, acting as *ecclesial subjects*. Patriarchy has taken charge of ecclesiality and denied it to lay people and particularly to women, alleging biblical, theological, and historical reasons that, as I have tried to show, are baseless. Re-appropriating ecclesiality involves the exercise of all freedoms and rights, which are indivisible and unrenounceable: the right of assembly, of association, of expression, of conscience, of investigation, of critique, of thought . . . and, above all, the right to dissent! This requires sharing in the government of the Christian community, a government elected and exercised democratically with no limitations. To achieve this, we need to set in motion a process of democratization of the church, which requires a change not only in its organization but also in its life. Considering all Christians, men and women as ecclesial subjects invalidates the distinction between clerics and laity, the teaching church and the learning church, the hierarchy and the people.

Women's citizenship has to extend into the sacramental sphere, in which we suffer a total exclusion through the androcentric conception that dominates this sphere. For this to happen, we women have to stop being mere receivers of grace and dumb hearers of the word and become mediators of salvation and interpreters of the word.

Together with full citizenship for women, we have to affirm the full citizenship of all those excluded by reasons of ethnicity, race, social class, geographical provenance or sexual preference. Citizenship should spread into a network, into an inclusive circle. This requires the union and solidarity of the excluded against the causes that bring about exclusion. The triad of Galatians 3.28 needs further amplification: 'no longer homosexual or heterosexual, no longer rich or poor, no longer white or black, no longer learned or unlearned . . .' Still respecting differences, of course, so as not to end up with a 'cloned' church and society.

Translated by Paul Burns

Notes

1. See E. Schüssler Fiorenza, *In Memory of Her. A Feminist Theological Reconstruction of Christian Origins*, New York 1983.
2. See E. W. and W. Stegemann, *Historia social del cristianismo. Los inicios del judaísmo y las comunidades cristianas en el mundo mediterráneo*, Estella 2001.
3. See K. Jo Torjesen, *Cuando las mujeres eran sacerdotes*,Córdoba 1996, pp.89–90.
4. This section is partly based on J. J. Tamayo-Acosta, 'Cuando las mujeres eran sacerdotes' in *El Pais* (Madrid), 10 July 2002.
5. V. Camps, *El siglo de las mujeres*. Madrid 1997, p.9.

A Woman's Right to Not Being Straight (El Derecho a no ser Derecha): On Theology, Church and Pornography

MARCELLA MARIA ALTHAUS-REID

'That was a kiss', he said.
'Was it really?' I asked in disbelief with my eyes still closed. 'I didn't feel anything.'
'There are many kinds of kisses.'
'What kind was that one?'
'Doesn't matter. We're talking mathematics here.'

James Cañón[1]

Sechem, the prince of the country, but a slave to his own lusts, took her and lay with her, it should be seen not so much by force as by surprise . . . See what came of Dinah's gadding: young women must learn to be chaste, keepers at home; *these properties are put together, Tit.ii.5, for those that are not keepers at home, expose their chastity.*

Matthew Henry[2]

I. On pornography and theology

Think pornography. Think about a pornographic image defined as offensive due to its quality of being static and detached. For instance, a woman's body used for advertising a brand of alcohol fixes and objectifies not only a body but sexuality too. Such fixity is almost of exegetical quality; it is the body interpreted because reification is an interpretation in itself. Even if pornographic images are in movement, like in an X-rated film, there seems to be a sense of confinement and stricture of sexual relationships. As with the protagonist of the story from Cañón, heterosexual ideology makes sure that in pornography kisses are reduced to a certain fixed order or taxonomy of desire. Any free, unprogrammed kiss will never be a kiss. There are many kinds of love and desire, but reflecting here on pornography as a hetero-sexual art, we can say that what is offensive is the repetitive mimicry pre-sented of one stereotypical desire. Unfortunately, the same can be said of Christian theology, which mimics the prevalent heterosexual ideology while excluding any epistemological attempt, which challenges its dualism, hier-archies and institutionalized gods.

Are there any free kisses in the church or in theology? Christian theology proclaims the grace of God as a gratuitous love given to human beings and creation. Yet, the free kisses from God seem to be reduced to the private aspect of faith more than to the public one. That is, sexual dissidents do not feel deprived of their communion with God, but from the churches. This happens because theology in an alliance with pornography as a method tends to work, like capitalism, with a hermeneutical circle of inverting identities. Marx has denounced in his critique of ideology as a method that ideas come first (in the sense of being valued and given preminence) while people as the real protagonists of history seem to come second. The hermeneutical circle of ideology makes of people followers of ideologies, instead of actors of history.[3] The point is that while human bodies became devalued things, and thus lovers in theology became devalued, high value and respect are given to things such as marriage for profit.

Pleasure is profit in theology for bartering purposes. For instance, there is a long tradition where pleasure is bartered with godly recompenses in Christian ethics. This is part of the exchange circle of forgiveness and the industry of confession. Therefore the need to construct the loving bodies as motionless bodies, that is, outside meaningful non-heterosexual relation-ships from which lessons of love can be learnt and more about the love of God can be discovered.[4]

According to Andrea Dworkin, pornography is an art of territorial occu-pation.[5] In theology, we may be also talking here of the politics of non-consensual heterosexual ideological interventions in the name of universal salvation. Yet, like in the unfortunate biblical commentary on Dinah by Henry, in heterosexual theology bodies easily become occupied territories, to be portrayed as faulty or sinful. If Dinah did not go out, she would not have been raped. By the same criteria, women who are not heterosexual should remain in their closets. The theo/logic here is one of claustrophobia.

II. On churches, capitalism and not being straight

We reflected briefly on pornography, and now we need to reflect more on theology. Capitalism, colonialism and pornography have many things in common with some kinds of theology. At least in the past they have had in common the essential characteristics such as the objectification of women, sexuality and the valorization of exploitative profit, such as when the family becomes abusive and women are discouraged from breaking their legal contracts in the name of God. Capitalism, colonialism and pornography always formed in a sense an ecumenical community, with territorial occupation as a goal and as a strategy. Today, with the global expansion of capitalism (*mundialización*) such adjudicated sexual roles in society may have changed, and even the hierarchical ordering of the world may have changed, but they still have a god-father in common; that is, the politically ever-expanding patriarchal god who does not recognize any kiss which has not been approved. For instance, in the present collapse of the Argentinian nation, the IMF has imposed economic laws for Argentina as a requisite to help the country in the extraordinary economic crisis which it is currently suffering. However, people know that such laws are only going to bring more hardship for a country where even pensions have been cut and old people are left to find food in rubbish tips. Therefore, they are organizing themselves into workers' co-operatives. Factories which have been closed down and abandoned have been taken by workers who organize themselves into co-operatives. They have not only succeeded in repairing the abandoned machines and distributing equal salaries amongst the workers, but they also allocate part of the monthly economic surplus for the benefit of the local communities. Yet, old-fashioned workers' co-operatives seem to be un-approved kisses for the IMF because they can lead my country into economic success but also a different political system. But global capitalism does not admit difference.

In the same way that workers in Argentina are looking for different ways in the economy instead of adapting or reforming the old ones, we can say that it is not that women need to claim their human rights in the church for the church to be reformed, but for the church to be radically transformed. Such transformation needs to be from a way of thinking God and the world which sexually and politically abuses people, and even God. God is the first casualty in theology if God becomes a puppet of heterosexual ideologies.

The combination of a sexually explicit position and that quality of fixity or immobility of the heavily conceptualized body may define a picture from a magazine or a text in the Bible as pornographic. Similar qualities, translated into an economic frame of thought, are also the characteristics of the IMF. However, these are ecclesiologies that seem to have more in common with the policies of the market than with the alternative society project of Jesus Christ. The market, for all its discourses on free competition and mobility, works on principles of presupposed immobility by trade agreements and regulations which allow exploitation to exist and to generate wealth for the empires. In Christianity, the heavily sexually restricted body of women seems to have produced the primordial ethos of theo/social confinement, that is the theology which has been done for the preservation and control of the imperial ideologies in power. In order to work, they require the immobility of women in sexual confinement, but such immobility is a heavily sexually conceptualized order. It is obvious that to talk about human rights and women in the church we need to start by querying if women have human rights in the church itself, but it is less obvious (but not less important) to consider which rights these are. For instance, are we talking here about rights of equality? And equal to whom? The right of *no ser derecha* or not to be straight[6] is not a human right based on equality but on difference; this is the right of the *other*, the right of people to be themselves, even if the doctrinary corpus ignores them. The time has come to recognize that a whole apparatus of pornographic, immobile definitions and fixed conceptualizations is responsible for the anthropological Babylonian captivity of the church that not only reduces people's lives and their vocation to no more than ideological definitions, but also reduces God. If God is to be found in human relationships of economic and loving orders, it is obvious that the right not to be straight in a capitalist society and church has the goal of liberating God.

However, blessed are the humble, for it takes nothing greater than the small gesture of a woman inclined to love another woman more than doctrines to destabilize the pornographic network of theology, based on the immobilization of identities and the reification of love.

III. Exegeting women's bodies

In theology we deal with pornography every day by working with texts depicting the sexual immobility of women and men in time and space in restricted, uncomfortable positions of a sexual and economic nature, as are found in many doctrinal positions. The woman's body, as depicted in theology, has constituted what we can call an exegetical body of women, that is, a body subjected to complicated exposition of origins and meanings of ideological heterosexual interpretation, basically an essentialized body subject to theological desires. This exegetical woman-body is problematic not necessarily because it has usually been built around the faulty biological construction of female identities from previous centuries, racial conceptualizations and different cultural understandings. Women, and *other* women (women from other races, cultures and time) are not the problem. The problem is not that the exegesis of women's bodies, of their desires and pleasures, are fixed in the Bible, but that they are caught in a heterosexual gaze which has been highly sacralized. More than the Bible, it is the eyes of the reader which are responsible for the construction of the imagined Christian woman's body; the illusory exegetical body of interpretation of what a woman is fixing, as it does, how that woman gets fulfillment in life. In this context the claim of so many women in the church, denouncing the brutality of patriarchal praxis has often been equivalent to the discourse of a 'no' meaning a 'yes'. The claim of her human rights becomes a claim to be recognized as human in the church but in order to succeed she would need to lose her faith in the church sexual ideological system. It is not the right to be a woman (as heterosexually defined) that needs to be claimed, but the right to be. It is interesting to consider that heterosexual women can only be liberated in the church by liberating the church of its sexual ideology. The right to 'not being straight' is the first to claim.

To reflect on issues of human rights in the church today means in a way to recognize the pornographic nature of Christian theology, and its characteristics of colonial expansion: bodies are occupied; identities fixed; women are objectified and the reflection on God deals more with ideology than with critical reality. Women as the actors of history and the actors of theology disappear as mere commodities of theological exchange. They become useful categories to organize a systematic theology around. For instance, in colonial theology grace, faithfulness and redemption were re-defined upon the background of a dialectic of imperial purity versus a sinful *other*. The *other* as the scapegoat of the sin of the masters was darker, more sinister, more sensual and lazy and less masculine emphasizing by contrast the abundant virile virtues of the Christian imperial power. The *other* was feminized. In a similar reversal mechanism, women's domestic drudgery became theological virtues in the church. Immobilizing women in the church according to patriarchal criterias has produced a tradition. The work done by theologians such as Elisabeth Schüssler Fiorenza[7] has an antipornographic nature. It destroys fixed, bound bodies of women in history by uncovering the movements and struggles of women in history.

The point is that women's bodies are prophetic not only because historically they denounce their confinement and announce the possibility of the alternative in our churches and society, but because they uncover the hidden spaces of theological struggles. Such spaces are sexual and economic ones. Women's exclusion or restricted inclusion in the churches and the economy are fundamental for the functioning of theological structures in control, such as racial and national claims and supremacies, and also economic configurations. From this perspective, it is not that the Bible is a pornographic text *per se*. Even allowing the pornographic language and violent sexual imagery of a book such as Hosea, what is pornographic is the theological mechanism that has not allowed the text to move on. Texts are not fixed because readers keep moving and even strong pornographic texts, as Hosea is, can be read not for the purpose of making an apology, but to destabilize it in order to find the core pornography of religion. Then, by a process of intertextuality, we could be reading to find, for instance, religion without heterosexuality. That is to say, that the church's eye is a pornographic eye which fixes the text of women and impedes not a re-reading but a re-writing of Hosea. For in order to use a non-pornographic reading, the text needs to recover its mobility and the contesting thrust of the bodies historically pinned down by sacred forces in theology.

IV. Women's rights and faith in sex

The point is that the church can never address issues concerning women's rights in the secular world until the doctrine of sex which is sustained by a pornographic theology has been declared illegal, and unrecognized kisses have become, by contrast, canonical. Until now the church has, no doubt, been supporting women's human rights but only according to the limitations of its own heterosexual fixed theological landscape. Churches vary in that. From women who cannot be ordained as priests, to women who still need to declare to their priests when they are having their periods in order to avoid polluting the sacrament of the eucharist, or the exclusion of non-heterosexual couples, there are many degrees and complexities of disrespect for human rights that only women know. Women's destinies and call to be more are daily aborted in many churches. One must not presuppose, though, that losing faith in the church's sexual project is a desirable project for lesbians, transvestites or bisexual women alone. On the contrary, considering the heterosexual appeal of churches and Christian theology alike, it should be also the task of heterosexual women to question the normativity and construction of women's identity in the churches and their 'fixity' in pornographic theology. As I have written elsewhere, the problem is that women (and especially poor women) tend to invest in the heteronormal project of the church in order to gain respect by default. The necessary and costly respect that those who are not free need.[8]

V. Prophetic bodies

I would like to refer to the Brazilian theologian Nancy Cardoso Pereyra and her seminal article on the body of women and prophecy in the Hebrew scriptures.[9] Cardoso Pereyra makes the point of finding prophecy in the Hebrew scriptures through the language of women's and children's oppressed bodies. For instance, the hunger of the poor becomes a prophetic voice denouncing the injustice of a society which did not distribute its resources equally. Women's bodies are also prophetic in the abuse they suffer. For instance, raped bodies speak of sex as dominion while a poor woman's body, such as that of Ruth's servant in the Hebrew scriptures, speaks of power and affection through her relation with Ruth herself. The violation of women's rights in the church are and have been historically denounced by the prophecy of women's bodies.

Women's suffering as prophetic seems to act by de-ideologizing sexual dogmatism in Christian theology. This is an important point, because what we are saying is that women's agency is not necessarily the conceptual understanding of triumph but that there is agency in exclusion. This happens especially when the excluded women's bodies surprise the church with their stubbornness. For instance, women loving women, or women challenging the heterosexual mythologies of contractual love between women and men, have been making it more and more difficult for the church to claim God as an hetero-ideologue of the oppressed. Claiming the right not to be straight is a contribution to the church and Christian theology because it uncovers the fact that many theological disputes are somehow disputes about women's bodies. If we agree with Paul Ricoeur that the concept of evil itself in Christian theology has been elaborated upon judicial and biological concepts of debt and inheritance,[10] we could start to consider how the conceptualization of women's bodies may be closer than anything else to the conceptualization of doctrinal bodies. How to think theology without pornography is the challenge that the question of women's rights in the church presents us by demanding that women's bodies cease to be doctrinally immobilized, stripped of their freedom and dignity and determined in their loving religious horizons.

At the core of any discussion on sexuality lies the threat of destabilizing dogmas and ecclesiologies which have made of God a resource of heterosexual authority. That requires the courage to find God outside sexual ideologies and ideologies of race and class. Sexual ideologies in particular are crucial in sustaining political ones, and women's rights inside and outside the church, as well God's rights, depend on how we confront them in what needs to be an alliance for more than one truth 'out of the closet' for heterosexual and non-heterosexual people alike. Meanwhile, God remains hidden by ideology. God also remains in the closet as a prisoner of the orthodoxy of theology and pornography, claiming for *'el derecho a no ser derecha'*, the right not to be straight in a church where the orthopraxis of love should be more important than its orthodoxy based on an uncritical position rooted on a (hetero-) sexual ideology.

Notes

1. James Cañón, 'My Lessons with Felipe' in Jaime Cortez (ed), *Virgins, Guerrillas & Locas. Gay Latinos Writing about Love*, San Francisco: Cleis Press 1999, p. 79.

2. Matthew Henry, *A Commentary on the Holy Bible*, vol. I, London: Marshall Brothers.

3. For a more detailed discussion on this point see my article '*¿Bién sonados?* The Future of Mystical Connections in Liberation Theology' in *Political Theology*, Issue 3, November 2000, pp. 44–63.

4. For a reflection on the contribution that lesbian theologies reflecting on love and relationship can make to the churches, see Elizabeth Stuart, *Just Good Friends*, London: Mowbray 1995.

5. See Andrea Dworkin, *Intercourse*, New York: Free Press 1987, p.133.

6. In Spanish, the word *'derecha/derecho'* can be translated as right, and also figuratively as straight.

7. Schüssler Fiorenza's original work has been precisely to restore the 'sense of movement' that women have in the history of the church, showing the instability of our concepts of women submission and passivity in the church. See, for instance, *Discipleship of Equals. A Critical Feminist Ekklesia-logy of Liberation*, New York: Crossroad and London: SCM Press 1993.

8. Marcella Althaus-Reid, *Indecent Theology*, London: Routledge 2000, ch. 2.

9. See Nancy Cardoso Pereyra, 'La Profecía y lo Cotidiano. La Mujer y el Niño en

el Ciclo del Profeta Eliseo' in *Revista de Interpretación Bíblica Latinoamericana*, 14, 1993, pp.7–23.

10. Cf Paul Ricoeur, *Le Conflit des Interpretations*, Paris: Editions du Seuil 1969, pp.265–82.

In God's Image: Theology in the Articulation of Women's Rights

LIEVE TROCH

Over the years feminist theology has worked in different ways on an articulation of women's rights, either by creating a theological legitimation for women's rights in their struggle for humanity or by taking this struggle as a theological starting-point for developing new theological images of the self, the world and God. Whereas the first line tends more towards sketching out universal concepts for the articulation of women's rights, the second offers more possibilities for articulating the diversity of the struggle in diversified theological language which does not define the situation but time and again opens it up anew. In this article I want to explore both lines briefly.

I. Feminist theology and the imago Dei: created in God's image?

In 1978 the theologian Carol Christ wrote a powerful article entitled 'Why Women Need the Goddess: Phenomenological, Psychological, and Political Reflections'.[1] She argues that there is a need for a different way of speaking of God as a condition for women to be able to develop to the full, and in order for it to be possible to put the power of women in a theological perspective. Mary Daly had earlier made it clear that since male images make up the essence of the divine, this automatically leads to the superiority of the male and gives divine legitimation to a deeply rooted sexism. The standpoints of the two authors refer to the twofold function which feminist theology gave itself from the beginning: on the one hand thinking critically through cultural expressions and constructions, and on the other hand reflecting in a critical feminist way on Christianity and its theological concepts.[2]

1. Reconstruction and unmasking

Since then, many womanist and feminist theologians have worked on the development of two important lines in feminist theological thought: on the one hand a reconstruction of the definition of the human subject and on the other a reconstruction of the depiction of the divine. They are intrinsically connected, and point to the traditional discussion of the *imago Dei* in theological anthropology. It is not in fact surprising that within Western feminist theology reflection on the *imago Dei* occupied an important place in women's struggle for their rights in the church and society and in claiming their rights as theological subjects. Women claim to be the complete image of God.

In theology the concept of the *imago Dei* points to the text of Gen.1.26–28, which states that man and woman, male and the female, are created in the image and likeness of God. In systematic theology the *imago Dei* has been used for reflection on the interaction between the depiction of God (image of God) and the definition of the human being (as image of God). This classical theological term also refers to the person and action of Christ as the perfect image of God.

We know a long tradition in the history of theology with discussions of whether women, too, are the image of God and as such can be fully recognized as co-creators. Since Paul already sowed the seeds of doubt on this question, various theologians have confirmed that women, too, bear the image of the divine being. By preference modern theology uses the categories of person and subject derived from the philosophical tradition in its exposition of human beings as the image of God.[3] Various feminist theologians have raised critical questions about the way in which the *imago Dei* has been defined throughout theology and has been claimed by the 'man'. Males have projected their longings and ideals on to the project. The interpretation of the *imago Dei* in which the likeness with God is seen above all in the spirit had and still has negative consequences for women, most of which are associated with corporeality, sexuality and earthiness. The result was a theological and actual contempt for women.

One of the great achievements of feminist analysis – not only in theology but in many of the humane sciences – is that it has unmasked the stereotypes of particular imaginary images of women as a projection of the male patriarchal consciousness. In addition it has also unmasked the current thought of Western philosophy and theology since Descartes in terms of subject as a pattern of thinking which puts a one-sided masculine white Western subject at the centre and excludes the imaginary images of women from it. In much later theology this Cartesian image of the human being was usually the starting-point for talking about the *imago Dei*. The feminist critique and reconstruction enriches this *imago Dei* in various ways. The discussions

about the *imago Dei* usually take place at three levels: those of sexual difference, the relationship between nature and human beings, and the problem
of immanence and transcendence, the sphere in which the image of God
especially applies.

Feminist theologians make a contribution by focussing attention on the
need for a link between the body, spirit and nature which was broken in the
classical theological definition of the *imago Dei*. They use this break to
explain the negative evaluation of corporeality in theology, the exclusion of
women and the destruction of nature.

2. Some examples

The theologian C. Halkes makes a reconstruction of the *imago Dei* which
refers back to the origin of the word in the framework of the theology of
creation. She puts the emphasis on a revaluation of creation, the equality of
men and women, and the connection between creation, incarnation and
eschaton.[4] She sees the *imago Dei*, which belongs equally to men and women,
in the first place as a task: the common task to which men and women are
called is to be the representative of God.[5] This role of representative
expresses itself in the task of continuing and preserving creation.[6] In this
process of becoming the *imago Dei*, men and women have to take different
ways, since they have different places within the patriarchal degeneration of
the world.

R. Radford Ruether uses being a complete human being as a critical
principle for defining the *imago Dei*; she couples this with authenticity and a
complete human potential. She combines it with the concepts of Christ and
redeemed humankind. This is not new, but in her view the new feature is
that these concepts are being claimed by women. She makes a distinction
between being potentially human and being historically human. Ruether
sees being historically human as a removal of the image of God. The unfolding of our complete human potential means the redemption of the *imago
Dei*. Our destiny as persons lies in complete humanity. Thus the *imago Dei*
functions as the depiction of the desire for what human beings should be;
what human beings should be in relation to the divine.[7]

The theologian H. Zorgdrager demonstrated earlier that the new feminist
constructions run the risk of being ahistorical and asexual and that they thus
reproduce the classical *imago Dei* discussion by once again thinking in metaphysical and essentialist categories.[8]

Another line is developed by M. Grey and a number of theologians who emphasize a new definition of the subject in terms of solidarity. This solidarity is seen as the deepest nature of human beings, in which everything is bound up with everything else; this can again be evoked and realized when we remember our origin. Here the connections which have been lost can be liberated once again. The privilege of this awareness of solidarity has repeatedly been associated with women and marginal groups. Grey fills in the characteristics and elements which belong with this sense of solidarity by using feminine metaphors like giving birth and being maternal.[9] Here the danger arises that women and groups on the periphery are seen as being 'better' than persons who on the basis of their nature and social location take it for granted that they should work towards just relationships.[10]

A. C. Mulder argues for a more bodily interpretation of the *imago Dei* as liberating for women by making use of the thought of L. Irigaray to present two subjectivities. She gives an interpretation of the concept of 'incarnation' which starts from the underivable difference between feminine and masculine bodily subjectivity and presents feminine subjectivity as being 'in the image of God'; consequently women need not be subject to the one norm.[11] Here she does not escape the danger of a new metaphysical construction with essentialist features. As in the previous authors mentioned, differences between and in concrete persons with their possibilities and limitations – which are expressed in concrete contexts in differences of power and structural patterns – are snowed under by these metaphysical ideals. The presentation of a new philosophical way of thinking in terms of the subject in accordance with the image of God as 'one or dual' is not in itself liberating for women and men. Liberation is brought about in self-chosen action for justice, in the fight against violence and oppressive powers. The subject constitutes itself in that action against imposed and pre-programmed identities and oppressive institutions.

II. Recreating the imago Dei – discipleship of equals

1. A remembrance kept alive

Already in the 1980s E. Schüssler Fiorenza developed a hermeneutic which declared the present company of women struggling for liberation to be the central starting point. She shifts attention from the androcentric biblical context to the social historical context through which in the Bible men and women are seen as victims and subjects in a patriarchal culture in which they struggle or do not struggle for democratic rights with the complete citizenship of everyone as the goal. Both the biblical texts and present-day experiences of struggle and joy offered openings here for constantly new theological notions. The Bible takes on the function of a prototype and does not serve to provide divine legitimation for the struggle. The *memoria passionis* of those who struggle for life against oppression and violence through history is the heritage of those who now once again try to make the face of God visible in the struggle.[12] This remembrance brings back lost lives from the margins and restores them to the centre, and is therefore subversive. Keeping the memory alive is not a legitimation for the struggle now but a powerful heritage which links past, present and future.

In this hermeneutic the focus is not on the redefinition of the subject as *imago Dei* nor in the fixing of the divine in an image. The social locations that bind each individual to structures of oppression which reinforce one another in many ways and which entangle individuals in them are the places where subjects make choices for liberation or for consolidation. The diversity of the fight for rights and full citizenship which follows from this shows a multiplicity of places and strategies for the struggle, a wide range of possibilities and limitations. In this conflictual movement towards equality, the 'discipleship of equals', revelation takes place and the vision of the kingdom, the *basileia*, is given. This multiplicity of positions and choices requires constant creative reformulation of the theologian in order to open up vistas on the divine which constantly retreat; vistas of an inclusivity which is called for by the struggle for democratic citizenship. The struggle over inclusivity and a surplus for all – the vision of the *basileia* (kingdom of God) – manifests itself differently in every culture, religion and social group. In this hermeneutic the multiplicity and diversity of changing subjects stands over against the unity or duality. Iconoclasm stands over against the making of images, the ongoing struggle of subjects who constantly recreate themselves in a conflictual dynamic over against the metaphysical ideal of an interconnected world. The concrete historical struggle constantly changes as a result of the patterns of oppression, which reconstruct themselves time and again.

2. *Two biblical stories*

To recall where the dominant *imago Dei* as an image of human beings and God has been shattered, and it is possible to see a counter-movement of subjects constituting themselves who had been driven to the periphery by oppressive subjects, I begin with two biblical stories. These are the stories of

Rizpah in II Samuel 21 and the girl friends of Jephthah's daughter in Judges 10 and 11. These texts took shape in the same period as the Genesis text on the *imago Dei*. Both texts have their context in stories of powerful men: David, who assumed messianic form, and the general Jephthah, who is later praised in the Letter to the Hebrews. The counter-movements are set in motion by a concubine, the slave girl Rizpah, and by a group of young girls.

The appearance of Rizpah (II Samuel 21) can be read as a sharp criticism of David's government. He exploits a situation of famine to settle an old score with Saul by sacrificing seven of his sons and grandsons to the Gideonites 'to gain God's favour'. The youths are hanged, and David does not allow them to be buried. The sacrifices are made to pacify a murmuring people which is asking for bread in a period of famine, and to disguise the lack of order in the distribution of the country's wealth. The 'heroes' have come to an agreement. And 'God' is brought in to explain and justify the problematical situation in which people are being manoeuvred. Among the seven men are two sons of Saul's concubine, the slave girl Rizpah. The text relates that the youths are killed in the first days of the harvest; the end of the famine was already recognized, unmasking the excuse for the murder.

Then in the story Rizpah appears: the slave girl, Saul's concubine, a third-rate figure used only to bear children. She rebels. Rizpah takes her mourning garb, her sackcloth, which she wears for her two dead sons, and spreads it out on a rock, on the mountain where her sons have been hanged. Rizpah continues to sit on the rock 'from the beginning of harvest until rain fell on them from the heavens'. In Israel at that time this represented a period of six months. For six months Rizpah keeps watch: she wards off the birds of prey and the beasts of prey that come after the corpses. Day and night, Rizpah goes to the limits and beyond the limits of what makes her position possible. She is not content with the God whom she encounters on the mountain through David. Her watch is a complaint, her presence a subversive power. She keeps the injustice in view. Rizpah's presence breaks the power of the messianic figure of David as the representative and image of God. Rizpah's sackcloth marks out the sphere for her protest; her own pain is the starting point and the place of her structural protest. In her power lies another image of the divine; she is the forerunner of many foolish men and women all over the world who know that justice begins with a long lonely fight against injustice. The long watch suggests the presence and support of many in order to give form to the counter-movement. The text reports that David repents. God did not die with the man on the mountain, but has become recognizable in a different form in Rizpah's protest.

In Judges 10–11 we are confronted with Jephthah, who in obedience to a promise to 'God' kills his daughter, still a child. Before the defenceless child is killed the text relates that she goes into the mountains with her girl friends for three months. This retreat of the girls has made her remembrance possible: 'So there arose an Israelite custom that for four days every year the daughters of Israel would go out to lament the daughter of Jephthah the Gileadite.' In both stories the *memoria passionis* is given a central place in a protest action. In this action another God shines out, made present by those who are defined by others in social structures of oppression, as a slave or as children not yet of age, but who themselves in turn take into their own hands the definition of themselves, the world and God.

3. Calls for opposition and transformation

In a parallel way, womanist theologians like K. Cannon and D. Williams shed light on the many forms of opposition from women in the time of slavery. K. Cannon seeks to name the 'virtues' which black women developed in order to make a way out of nothingness. These women did not derive their values and norms from the white society which made them non-persons, but showed a moral wisdom that put them in a position to survive while maintaining their integrity. When Cannon goes on to speak of what she calls 'mining the mother lode', she speaks of invisible wisdom and quiet grace. Quiet grace is the quest for truth and is to be found in the power of black songs, stories and sayings in which the lie is given to the truth of the whites and the presuppositions of white truth which are fatal for blacks are rejected.[13] D. Williams arrives at a radical restatement of the function of redemption by reflecting on the pain, the suffering and the opposition of black women.[14]

The *mujerista* theologian A. Maria Isasi Diaz formulates the power of Latina women in the United States in a variety of perspectives for action: the struggle, finding a voice, and commitment to the community as constitutive factors of their existence and the starting point for their theology.[15]

Since the beginning of the 1980s the journal *In God's Image* has been appearing four times a year.[16] It presents itself as a journal which gives women in Asia the opportunity to allow their theological voice to be heard. It is a colourful collection of texts which differ in style and content. From the various Asian contexts, cultures and lands accounts are given of events and topics which define the daily life of Asian women and the way in which Asian women operate as subjects within it. Alternative networks are presented, and in creative ways an account is given of meetings and conferences. *In God's Image* is the place where many Asian women make their voices heard in the midst of diverse forms of oppression, where they struggle and play before God's face.

These prototypical counter-voices, open to an ever-new transformation in a complex web of oppression, constantly recreate the vision. The struggle for a discipleship of equals involves conflict. In that work of transformation sometimes the face of God shines out in the bearers of the image, who create beauty and grace in a variety of colours. The divine can be attained in the protest of broken bodies, bodies broken by hunger, violence, cultural and religious restrictions. God's image is time and again recreated by victims and non-persons who recreate themselves in a diverse struggle for recognition and complete citizenship. God's image, the *imago Dei*, becomes visible, to disappear again on the horizon where the vision calls.

Translated by John Bowden

Notes

1. C. Christ, 'Why Women Need the Goddess: Phenomenological, Psychological, and Political Reflections' in C. Christ and J. Plaskow (eds), *Womanspirit Rising. A Feminist Reader in Religion*, 1979, pp.273–87.
2. Anne E. Carr, *Transforming Grace: Christian Tradition and Women's Experience*, San Francisco 1988, p.99.
3. For an argument on this see H. Zorgdrager, 'Feministische theologie over het imago Dei, een nieuw Paradigma' in J. Huisman and S. de Jong (eds), *Immanentie/Transcendentie. Congresbundel Theologie van IWEV-congres Overgrenzen: Vrouwen en wetenschappelijke innovaties*, Ru Groningen 1989, pp.113–32.
4. C. Halkes, . . . *en alles zal worden herschapen. Gedachten over de heelwording van de schepping in het spanningsveld tussen natuur en cultuur*, Baarn 1989, p.159.
5. This representation motivates her to put the Genesis text in the royal ideology: C. Halkes, *Oorsprong en Einder, Cultuurkritische overwegingen vanuit vrouwenstudies theologie*, Baarn 1995, p.115.
6. Ibid., pp.115–17.
7. For an extended discussion of the *imago Dei* in Ruether see A. Mulder, 'Imago Dei: De Mens (M/V) of "man" en "Vrouw" als beeld van God. Het mensbeeld van R-R. Ruether bekeken vanuit het denken van L. Irigaray' in F. Dröes et al. (eds), *Proeven van vrouwenstudies theologie III*, Zoetermeer 1993, pp.17–42, above all pp.34 and 39.
8. Zorgdrager, 'Feministische theologie' (n.3), pp.126–7.

9. M. Grey, *The Wisdom of Fools? Seeking Revelation for Today*, London 1993, pp.87–90, 116; ead., *Redeeming the Dream. Feminism, Redemption and Christian Tradition*, London 1989, pp.138–43.

10. For a more extended evaluation of these forms of subject thinking see L. Troch, *Verzet is het geheim van de vreugde. Fundamentaaltheologische thema's in een feministische discussie*, Zoetermeer 1996, pp.7–95.

11. A. Mulder, *Divine Flesh, Embodied Word. Incarnation as a Hermeneutical Key to a Feminist Theologian's Reading of Luce Irigaray's work*, Utrecht 2000.

12. E. Schüssler Fiorenza, *In Memory of Her. A Feminist Theological Reconstruction of Christian Origins*, New York and London 1983, pp.30–36, 92; ead., *Bread Not Stone. The Challenge of Feminist Biblical Interpretation*, Boston 1984, xvi-xvii; ead., *But She Said. Feminist Practices of Biblical Interpretation*, Boston 1992.

13. K. Cannon, *Black Womanist Ethics: Resources for a Constructive Ethic in the Life and the Work of Zora Neal Hurston*, Atlanta 1988; L. Troch, 'Als een Fenix oprijzend uit de as. K. G. Cannon en het womanisine' in *Mara. Tijdschrift voor feminisme en theologie* 3, 1990, vol. 3, p.21.

14. D. Williams, 'Black Women's Surrogacy Experience and the Christian Notion of Redemption' in Cooey, Eakin and McDaniel (eds), *After Patriarchy. Feminist Transformations of the World Religions*, New York 1991, pp.1–14. See also D. Williams, 'Women's Oppression and Life-Line Politics in Black Women's Religious Narratives', *Journal of Feminist Studies in Religion* 1, 1985, 2, pp.59–71.

15. A. M. Isasi Diaz, 'Elements of a Mujerista Anthropology' in A. O'Hua Graff (ed), *In the Embrace of God. Feminist Approaches to Theological Anthropology*, pp.90–102.

16. *In God's Image*, Journal of Asian Women's Resource Centre for Culture and Theology.

Inter-Religious and Inter-Cultural Work for Women's Rights

MARGARET SHANTHI STEPHENS

Introduction

In the recent past a young Catholic woman, who had eloped with and married a Muslim, approached me with the problem of settlement of their inter-religious marriage. To my suggestion that they register their marriage in the civil court as the best option, she explained that her husband preferred marriage according to Muslim Shariah law and only then would he agree to register the marriage in a civil court. Her hesitation rested on her fear that after such a Shariah marriage, he would divorce her, as that was his mother's wishes. Secondly, when she approached the parish priest, he wished to meet and convert her Muslim husband to the Catholic faith. She was in a dilemma or trauma, as the rights and obligations of the parties vary a great deal under the two diverse laws.

In both Islam and Christianity, the religious and theological structures seem to be a burden to young couples whose love marriages face the issue of adherence to either one religion wherein the woman's situation is most vulnerable, or move towards inter-religious dialogue to live in harmony. In both Islam and Christianity, the interpretation of scripture texts and marriage-related laws remain solely in the hands of male priests and theologians. Asghar Ali Engineer, at a seminar on 'Muslim Women: Rights and Empowerment', stated that the interpretation of the Qur'anic texts by theologians was the real problem and in the context, there was a need for female theologians. The same can be said for Christianity as well. In both these traditions women are easily victimized.

In India/Asia any action for liberation of women demands inter-religious and inter-cultural work for women's rights! The masses of the world's poor live in India/Asia, which is also the womb of many religions and cultures. Aloysius Pieris defines the Asian character of Third World Theology as 'poverty and religiosity'. To our specific Indian context I would add, 'caste and patriarchy'. The Indian/Asian context is interwoven with a complexity of forces operative that affect the poor, especially women. While liberal capitalism and globalization are dominant forces in the world economy, it has adverse effects on the majority poor, particularly women. The feminization of poverty and of labour clearly point to the fact that both the poor and labour have a markedly 'woman's face'! However, feminist research has to probe further into the non-economic aspects, namely, the religion-caste-patriarchy nexus in its analysis of the roots of women's subordination and exploitation.

I. Women's organizations and religious/theological structures

In the past most women's organizations rejected religion as one of the main causes of women's oppression. 'Women, as primary victims of orthodox religion, have good reason to be resentful of religion in general.' Confronted by the rise in religious fundamentalism, religious revivalism and especially the many communal conflicts and riots both nationally and internationally, wherein women are the worst affected, recently there is a significant shift in women's organizations realizing the urgent need of women's role in religious reform. In the recent riots and massacre of innocent people in Gujarat unleashed by Hindutva forces and supported by the state government, masses of raped women were unable to file an FIR; instead the government reports show only three registered cases of rape. A Muslim woman, Amina Aapa, witnessed the rape of a woman, Kauser Bano, who was nine months pregnant. 'Her unborn baby was slashed out of her womb before being tossed into the fire to be roasted alive. Thereafter she too was brutally cut up and torched. There is not a single woman resident of Hussain Nagar whose dignity was left intact.' The growing 'intolerance and hate campaign' are indicators of the religious-political forces that have unleashed violence and death, and these have to be understood and strategies evolved to sustain women's lives.

All liberative struggles for women's rights or against violence done to women have to be inter-religious and inter-cultural, given the context of religious and cultural diversities. We shall consider the contemporary Indian context, especially the phenomenon of religious revivalism and its consequences for women, to create positive strategies and make an action plan in the struggle for women's rights.

II. Religious revivalism – politicization of religion

While peoples of diverse religious faiths wish to live in harmony with each other, all around us are signs of the growing religious resurgence and intolerance nationally and internationally: Hindutva forces strive to insti-gate a 'hate campaign' in their bid to make India a Hindu theocratic state; militant Muslims proclaim *jihad* and instill fear as terrorists; and church leaders hold on to their fundamentalist position proclaiming the uniqueness of Jesus Christ through the document, 'Dominus Jesus'.

Within the majority religion – Hinduism – early Hindu revivalists were apolitical, inclusive in their approach and displayed no anti-minority or communal stand. On the other hand, the later ethnic nationalism was clearly a political struggle that sought to use religion as the basis of the emerging identity of India. The latter had taken on a distinctively commu-nal, right-wing identity that was exclusive and anti-minority in its approach. It sought a definition of Hinduism that was clearly political, i.e. a religious syndicalism for political purposes, an exclusive Hindu-ness and a rejection of non-Hindus – all of which were absent in Hindu revivalism. According to Savarkar, Muslims and Christians looked outside India for the sacred places of their religion and therefore did not regard India as their holy land. In defining Hindu nationality he underlined the importance of Hindutva, a religious, racial and cultural entity.

Developing nations and cultures experience the search for 'multi-culturalism' on the one hand and aggressive reaction on the other, through militant religious fundamentalism. Scholars conclude that the resurgence of religious fundamentalism is a reaction against the threatening features of globalization, through its economic and political neo-colonialism. These movements in their strong rejections have taken to political and violent militant forms of reactions. We have the example of Robertson, who earlier thought religious resurgence was a reaction to the process of globalization. But his recent analysis asserts a change in his religious–political approach where he sees religious fundamentalism as a creation of globalization.

More importantly, these fundamentalist movements that reject global culture as neo-colonial seem to strengthen a version of traditional culture that is hierarchical, fundamentalist and determinedly patriarchal. They not only reject minority religions (Christianity, Islam) as culturally 'foreign', but they practice an internal dominance over their women, enforcing stringent measures to keep them in subservience because they are 'women'. Women's experiences of male control by the Taliban in Afghanistan and militant outfits both in Jammu-Kashmir in the West and in Mizoram in the East in the recent past, and the atrocities perpetrated on women of minority communities in Gujarat testify to the oppressive condition of women.

III. Role of religions/church

As an Indian Catholic woman, living amidst diverse faiths, I believe a critical feminist consciousness implies and demands an evaluation of the role and influence of religions, particularly Roman Catholicism in maintaining the status quo and in preventing wo/men from gaining their full human rights. In India/Asia the church has been hand in glove with the colonizers in their imperialist dominance: not only in extracting the wealth of the South and creating poverty, but in the imposition of cultural apartheid. The impact of colonization, especially the denigration of Hindu religion (idolatry, superstitious, polytheistic) aroused a strong reaction as well as realization in Indian intellectuals of the cultural and ideological implications of colonialism. This required Indians to be both imitative of and hostile to the model they sought to imitate; both to reject the alien intruder and dominator and also to accept its ways and what it had to offer. This led to a search for an identity of India in opposition to the Western colonial and materialistic culture, to maintain an essential spiritual quality.

The insight – to be religious is to be inter-religious – expresses the need to go beyond, understanding other faiths as the 'other', what Panikkar terms as 'intra-religious'. One of the recent accusations against Roman Catholicism by the Hindu fundamentalists is the lack of inculturation, that the church still remains 'foreign'. I believe that the church, instead of being defensive, has to shed the 'Roman' label, become truly local church, and seek ways to dialogue with the diverse indigenous religions/cultures, its symbols, and particularly its communitarian values. Authentic dialogue and deep inculturation take place only if we are prepared to be 'baptized in the Jordan of Asian religiosity' and 'crucified in the Calvary of Asian poverty'. The Catholic church has to move consciously away from its inculturation of dominant Hindu culture, marked by casteism and misogynism to be closer to God's reign. Specifically its oppressive 'purity-pollution' norms have excluded dalits as 'untouchables' and women from official leadership roles and theological production. Such oppressive characteristics are alive among the church's members, its choice of leaders, bishops, theology, etc.

At the Asian Bishops Conference (FABC) held at Samphran, Thailand, from 3–13 January 2000, the participants insisted the church cannot be a sign of the kingdom and of the eschatological community if the fruits of the spirit to wo/men are not given due recognition, and if women do not share in 'the freedom of the children of God'. However they did not address issues as exclusion of women from official leadership roles, or exploitation of wo/men (religious women) in the church as cheap labour force/ sexuality. The church takes for granted that men represent the church and have no qualms of conscience that women are still invisible in leadership and theological production. As Fiorenza says, 'Because of this andro-kyriocentric assumption in theological discourses, the catholicity of ekklesia understood as a radical democratic congress of fully entitled, responsible decision making citizens has never been fully realized either in church history or in Western democracy.' The church must renew/reconstruct its ecclesial symbolism to be true to Jesus' counter-cultural movement symbolized by table-fellowship (Matt.22.1–10).

IV. Women's oppression – complex inter-structuring

The experience of the poor oppressed women is the locus and also the source of feminist liberation theologies. Feminist theologies grow out of women's struggles and sufferings, women's stories and myths, persecutions and protests as well as their dreams and visions. Women's experience of inequality and violence in a contemporary Indian/Asian women's context indicates a very strong link between the economic and religious-cultural factors. While it is people who organize the economy, we need to realize that they are guided by world-views, values and perspectives that are religious and cultural. Culture, as a symbolic whole of world-views, has a deep influence on economy, while religion as the deepest element of culture deals with the ultimate goal of life. Hence the complicity of economics, religion and culture, which is dominantly patriarchal, have a negative influence on women.

While every religion has its own specific goal, meaning system, religious symbols and orientation, inequality and violence against women within its structures cuts across religious and cultural divide. Such a situation is enhanced by the socio-cultural and even economic structures, reinforced through religious symbolic structures as well. Feminist theory has to move away from conceptualizing patriarchy in terms of gender oppression and male-female dualisms. Rather the feminist discourse has to study in depth the complex inter-structuring of sexism, class and caste exploitation, racism, and neo-colonialism (globalization and liberalization) in maintaining women's unequal status and subordinate role legitimized by religions.

Theological deconstruction leading to reconstruction is essential for women's struggles against sexism. It includes a critical review of God, who is not only male but hierarchical and absolute. Fiorenza names it 'kyriarchy'. In her critique of the church, she argues the need not only to deconstruct its obvious eurocentrism but also its pervasive andro-kyriocentrism. 'The absence of women from the ranks of bishops is not just an historical accident but the result of systemic discrimination and legal exclusion; it is due to the structural sin of misogyny and its theological rationalizations. As long as women are excluded from church leadership and governance not just by custom but also by law, the catholicity of the world-church is jeopardized. Hence the exclusion of wo/men from full ekklesial citizenship with all rights and responsibilities is not just a "woman's question" but a fundamental theological problem.'

Deconstructing is therefore to be understood as a breaking down of the established patriarchal mindset, disqualifying its claims of universality. Deconstruction includes the possibility of reconstructing new models that can subvert the sexist, racist, or colonial dynamics present in traditional theology and culture, so that the marginalized in indigenous cultures and religions, particularly women, can find their true place. The reason why I see this need for theological deconstruction is especially because the process of globalization includes an agenda of cultural homogenization, which sets itself above all other cultures, seeking to destroy the richness and diversity specific to each people, their religion and culture.

V. Beyond religions – women bonding

When women have a felt need of coming together to meet and share their experiences as 'woman' – a point of significance – women are ready to privatize their personal religious affiliations. Among the varied women's organizations, from right wing and traditional groups to communist or leftist women's organizations, the latter strive to link women's liberation and class struggle inclusive of masses of grassroots women vendors, casual labourers, etc. Yet, these have to still integrate women's issues beyond 'class interests' with the question of religion, culture and patriarchy. When analysing the material base of women's exploitation, we cannot limit ourselves to critique of capitalism alone, but have to include women's sexuality as the site of manipulation, violation and exploitation, which is culturally and religiously monitored. This is so at the personal and collective level, wherein women's labour, fertility and sexuality are exploited. The autonomous women's movements have helped through their analysis to include larger groups of women because of women's issues as abortion, health care, rape or dowry and recently the question of 'patriarchy in religions' against the background of communalism and its effects on women.

From my experience of belonging to an autonomous women's organization here in Tamilnadu, India, of importance is the growing interest in religion and spirituality. Women from different religious traditions, or women who have moved away from practising religion, or are atheists, etc., all come under one umbrella – 'woman'. Quite consciously women have felt the need to talk about their personal religious affiliations and the need to not only keep it private but be willing to critique it in the interests of sustaining ourselves as a 'women's organization'. The growing atrocities and violence against women become a matter of grave concern when it turns communal. We have to view patriarchy not as a separate entity, but recognize how it is intrinsically embedded within the very structures of capitalism, religious traditions and cultures.

In the latter approach the 'woman's question' becomes the point of encounter in the search for relevant aspects in each religious tradition, which is supportive of women's rights. The quest for liberative elements in religion can be the special focus, for this brings us to the very inter-religious and inter-cultural structures, the point that brings women together as 'woman'.

VI. Women-centred culture

A culture of dominance embedded within religions and theological structures have so conditioned women to be receivers and carriers of patriarchal culture. These are psychological manipulations that keep intact the social order, structure consciousness and form subjectivities, demanding compliance. Thus social behaviour is engineered through conformity and fear sanctioned by religion. It is imperative women deconstruct these and reconstruct creatively or revolutionize new cultural paradigms. Culture implies a specific way of looking at the human in society, the goals of life, religion and ethics, the values and attitudes that govern individual and social behaviour, for these affect the multi-cultural context of India. These cultural forces of modernity and post-modernity are materialistic, secularizing, fragmenting, dehumanizing and destructive of communitarian values, treating women as 'sex-objects, commodity and non-persons'. Feminists have always drawn attention to the ways in which patriarchal culture constructs 'norms of femininity' into which women are socialized and within which they are disciplined.

Critical analysis of the male bias of mainstream culture and its related denigration of all that is coded as 'feminine' will bring to visibility the many little ways in which marginalized women (poor, dalit, tribals, etc.) become cultural modifiers, through which they show resistance, as well as protest. These indicate women's assertion of their 'selfhood'. Oppressed women's covert or open resistance points to the fact that resistance is a sign of nascent power, which is needed to change the discourse. However, emphasis on a woman-centred culture to be constructed rather than on a feminine culture to be retrieved is important here, although it still leaves open what feminists/women share. Feminists point out the rich cultural variety of women's creativity and cultural diversity of feminine identities.

Conclusion

Change or transformation is desired by those committed to empowerment of women, by women themselves, in the thirst for their rights and identity as 'woman' and 'human' persons. The church of the poor, women-church, and all oppressed peoples are beginning to bond together, understanding the power of collective identity. I would like to conclude with a sign of hope from Muslim women who met the All-India Muslim Personal Law Board in Delhi on 7–8 April 2001 to discuss issues of genuine concern to Muslim women, with a public hearing. The Ulema willingly listened to many Muslim women, social actions groups, etc. When will such a dialogue be possible in a church that claims catholicity?

DOCUMENTATION

Recent Notifications on the Works of Reinhard Messner, Jacques Dupuis and Marciano Vidal

ALBERTO MELLONI

On 15 May 2001 *L'Osservatore Romano* published the 'Notification on some writings of Fr Marciano Vidal CSSR'. It was the third such intervention published by the Congregation for the Doctrine of Faith in the months between the end of the jubilee and the public consistory of 2001. In the period between December 2000 and May 2001, the Congregation intervened to clarify the 'doctrines' contained in the Austrian scholar Reinhard Messner's dissertation on 'Martin Luther's Reform of the Mass and the Eucharist of the Early Church: A Contribution towards a Systematic Liturgiology' and his Habilitation thesis on 'Celebrating Conversion and Reconciliation' (Notification of 6 December); in the manual *Towards a Christian Theology of Religious Pluralism* by the theologian Jacques Dupuis SJ (notification of 24 January 2001); and most recently in the volume *Moral de actitudes* and the *Dictionary of Theological Ethics. The Moral Teaching of John Paul II. Theological and Moral Commentary on the Encyclical* Veritatis Splendor, by Marciano Vidal (Notification of 22 February 2001). Around these interventions there have been others which would be worth studying in order to understand better the action of a Congregation which is so crucial in the life of the church and in its relations with other churches.[1]

However, by the route by which they come out, by the character of the three authors, and by the rapid sequence in which they have arisen, these Notifications already raise some questions:

1. Who is in fact trying to take a detached look at such actions?
2. What are the great historical models by which, willy-nilly, the ex-Holy Office seeks to measure itself?
3. Despite the concern of Paul VI to reform method and aims, is the discomfort which such 'clarificatory' procedures cause a necessary evil?
4. Have the notifications by the Congregation become a real danger or are

'exemplary' cases being made because of the weaknesses or the interests of the institution which promulgates them?

5. Is there a mistrust of the bishops, whose authority is invoked and worn down at the same time?

6. Does the decision to accuse these authors of 'ambiguity' not derive from the disputes over the magisterium triggered off in the middle of the 1980s and on the kind of expression on which it seems to want to make moral theology, communion and discipline depend?

In short, there are increasingly marked contradictions within and around the procedures, and from a historical point of view it is not easy to identify who benefits from them. I shall take up these questions in order.

1. A detached look

As I have said, we have to put the utmost emphasis on these questions if we are not to be prisoners of the simplification of the media, which (while being of some interest to public opinion and enjoying some confidence from the church in its use of communication as a key to power), emphasize the emotive side and ignore the historical depth of the decisions of the Congregation. The mechanisms of journalism tend to identify these decisions with the will of its head (to the point of using the name 'Ratzinger' as synonymous with the Congregation). They say nothing about the many defeats suffered by those preparing proceedings because of the determination of some bishop jealous of his responsibility;[2] they underestimate the internal dialectic and the antagonisms which run through the Roman world of the 'curia';[3] and they reduce to an antimodernist cipher procedures which deserve greater attention.[4]

For those who want to (or can) take a detached look at the decisions which emerge from the palace on the Piazza Cavalleggeri, another approach is possible. While respecting to the maximum the indignation or the satisfaction that the interventions of the Congregation of the Doctrine of Faith produce, this approach in the long term makes it possible to put in question the short *histoire immédiate* of the doctrinal controversies in Roman Catholicism. It is possible to adopt this approach today because there are quite important historical studies through which one can set all the decisions (including the three most recent ones) for which Joseph Ratzinger has assumed responsibility before the pope and the church against a deeper background. Here I do not want to present more than a report, nor can I; however, I think that three historiographical results have to be recalled.

2. Three historical models

The first comes from researches into the origins of the Holy Office, the protagonists of which are, among others, Adriano Prosperi and Elena Brambilla. Thanks to them one fact has now been established critically: after its institution in 1542, the first struggle of the Holy Office, which to a certain degree permanently determined its institutional stamp, was not solely or generically against the heretics; it was a struggle in Rome against milieux and persons alien to that culture which wanted to govern the world by controlling or defending consciences. The historians have shown that in some great processes (from that of Cardinal Giovanni Morone to that against Cardinal Reginald Pole) the organ of the Inquisition acquired a power which became determinative in filtering access to the pope 'by means of appropriate dossiers' produced by its 'secret police'.[5] Such studies on the origins of the Holy Office together with the recent opening up of its archives allow a reading from within of the actions of the Congregation which became 'supreme' – though of course these are works which run the risk of becoming 'wedded to the logic' which has produced such actions and thus of assuming a perspective which is fatally orientated on justification.[6] However, I believe that these analytical excavations allow us to understand better and better the weight of conceptions, antagonisms, nuances, practices, exceptions and mentalities which by its very existence this institution introduces into essential parts and dimensions of the Christian life.[7]

The work of the historians of the anti-modernist repression at the beginning of the twentieth century is just as important for grasping a second paradigm at work in the action of the Congregation for the Doctrine of Faith. As Pierre Colin has shown admirably and as the documents from the secret Vatican archive on the pontificate of Pius X, courageously made available by the reigning pope,[8] demonstrate with increasing clarity, between 1903 and 1914 an 'authentic' fear for the purity of the Catholic faith allowed the establishment of mechanisms of intimidation and informing on a vast scale: this apparatus of intellectual repression which marks the years preceding the First World War would take a decade to dismantle.[9] And beyond that date this phobia, with its disproportionate dangers and signals, weakened theological knowledge and episcopal authority at the end of the 1920s and early 1930s, when the church found itself fatally involved in the dramas of the time.[10]

Finally, contemporary historians have investigated a third archetype which has long been effective in the functioning of the Holy Office – it is expressed in the crisis in the relationships between theology and the magisterium in post-war Europe which came to a climax with the condemnation of the *nouvelle théologie*. It was above all Étienne Foulloux, with his highly accurate reconstructions of the persecutions of the Jesuit fathers of Lyons[11] and his work on the atmosphere of the Dominican province of France,[12] and finally the publication of the *Journal d'un théologien 1946–1956* of Yves Congar, which documented the depths of a repression within the church imposed with totalitarian methods (the impenetrability of procedures, the lack of guarantees, the use of psychological torture) of such a kind as to justify the future cardinal Congar in using the term Gestapo of the Holy Office.[13]

3. Reform of the institution and of procedures

It is well known that Paul VI intervened to reform the curia and also the 'supreme' Congregation – strikingly, immediately after Vatican II:[14] the pope's action – a solitary one, performed without the support of the Council, which had merely raised the question through a famous speech by Cardinal Frings on 8 November 1963[15] – had a threefold aim.

On the one hand it put the Secretary of State above the curial machine and subordinated the new Congregation for the Doctrine of Faith to him; the Congregation thus lost that function of control (its ancient name called it 'supreme and universal') which could have forced itself within the mechanisms of the conclave. Pope Montini, abolishing the baneful name of 'Holy Office', aimed at making a break with methods and practices which had been the cause of bitter shame for the Catholic Church. At the same time he maintained the centralization of a function of doctrinal control which for centuries constituted a factor of tension between local bodies, religious orders and the Roman centre.

The balance between these authorities has been realized, upset and corrected in the practice of the Congregation thus reformed, whether on the level of specific political action by the Office,[16] by the alternation of the two prefects (Seper from 1968 to 1981, Ratzinger from 1981 to the present),[17] by the selection and in the turnover of collaborators, or by the production of documentation.[18]After the promulgation of the new *Codex Juris Canonici* and the third reform of the Roman curia, John Paul II approved a normative structure which is contained in the *Regolamento proprio della Congregazione per la Dottrina della Fede*. The part which is of interest to us is contained in the *Ratio agendi in doctrinarum examine* of 30 May 1997. These are documents in which some rights of those being investigated are stated (perhaps one might say amplified):[19] however, only the historical research mentioned above makes it possible to say what elements in the decisions of the Congregation for the Doctrine of Faith continue to activate remote archetypes, demands for continuity which are essential for grasping its depth and historical nature without lapsing into the simplified popularization of those who approve or disapprove of it.

Taken together, the notifications on Messner, Dupuis and Vidal allow us to check at close quarters the way in which the rule has been used and when (after the bunch of decisions which run from the *Professio fidei* of 1989 to the *motu proprio Ad tuendam fidem*[20]) the Congregation declares a book to be dangerous for the Catholic faith. I do not in fact intend to go in to the merits of the problems discussed between three theologians and the Congregation – all the more so since in all three cases the procedure of the notification attests and documents the efforts that those under suspicion have made to meet the requests made to them. I shall limit myself to investigating the formal aspects which emerge from the notifications, which are not external or marginal, on the hypothesis that these questions can produce contradictions, tendencies and objectives which are not otherwise evident.

4. A necessary evil?

First of all I think that the serious effort made by the Congregation to distinguish between *authors* and *writings* needs to be noted and considered. The Congregation states that it wants to prevent the harmful effects of writings, and does not intend to cast a shadow or to discredit the persons of the authors. This is something new. It is enough to re-read the 1972 Declaration against Piet Schoonenberg or that against Hans Küng the next year,[21] or the investigation into Edward Schillebeeckx, to find a way of talking which aimed at striking just as much against the errors of the men, or to turn to the 1985 notification against Leonardo Boff[22] and the whole document on liberation theology, which sought to isolate men in the front line in the struggle for justice together with their writings. Even in 1987, the Congregation had retorted in a somewhat scornful way to Charles E. Curran, who had asked who his accusers were, that 'his works were his accusers'.[23] We could also move on and recall the harsh standpoint adopted against Christian Duquoc's *Des églises provisoires* (1985) and above all the incredible hardships arising for Jean-Marie R. Tillard because of his *Église d'Églises*. Here is a theologian of exemplary dedication in ecumenical dialogue and the author of the memorable speech made by John Paul II to the World Council of Churches in Geneva, but that is not enough to quote to defend him from the suspicions expressed in a deliberately defamatory way.

As I have said, in 2000 the tone is quite different. The Congregation not only recognizes 'valid stimuli' in the works of Messner but states that it does not consider it 'its task to investigate the historical and systematic-theological discussions which appear within the books': it also wants to 'leave open the purely theological questions' (*sic*), limiting itself to recalling the doctrines of faith which must be firmly held. On the topic of the theology of religious pluralism, too, the Congregation recognizes the 'willingness to provide clarifications' immediately shown by Fr Dupuis and states that it does not want to pass 'judgment on the subjective thought of the author', recognizing that his 'intentions' can be good. Finally, in the case of Vidal the notification admits that it is in the presence of an author who is 'disposed to clarify' the positions he has taken and recognizes that the 'principles confessed by the author' are healthy.

However, quite apart from the tone, the public actions of the Congregation have an effect which is punitive even before the problems (whatever they are) are clarified. Precisely as in the inquisitorial process of excommunication 'it is a summons to appear which contains confused elements of procedure and punishment'.[24] And precisely as in many anti-modernist proceedings, the submission of the guilty party ('*laudabiliter se subiecit*' is the ancient formula of the Holy Office) does not prevent the punishment, but is the basis for it – just as with these historical precedents the notification is already a punishment which affects a person. The feeling that Yves Congar had in 1956 perhaps always applies to everyone. 'They have not touched my body; in principle they have not touched my soul. They have asked nothing of me. But the person of a man is not limited to his skin and his soul. Above all when this man is a doctrinal apostle, he *is* his action, he *is* his friendships, his relations, he *is* his normal influence.'[25]

The notification sets out to sterilize the denigratory effects; it does not in any way amount to a condemnation, nor does it judge intentions, but with its material development it acts as a punishment on people's reputations,[26] and excludes them from the fundamental right to communicate their own intentions in the authenticity of the Christian communion. Is it a necessary evil *ad tuendam fidem?*

5. An inevitable disparity?

It also seems to me to have been demonstrated that the beginning of the examination of the doctrines of a work which culminates, as it has done recently, in the notification does not succeed in preventing the author accused from suffering objective detriment to his rights, despite the quest for bureaucratic consistency provided for by the *Ratio agendi.* No one guarantees (or can guarantee) that the questions raised will be examined for what they are and not for what they can become in an uncontrollable theological and ecclesial context. As an example, it is enough to note that in the twenty-seven months which have passed between the communication to Messner of the first series of criticisms of his dissertation by the Congregation (there is no point in seeking explanations for this) and the publication of the notification in the *Osservatore Romano*, the Catholic-Lutheran dialogue has made a leap forward with the confirmation of the Augsburg agreement on justification.[27] The study of the controversy with Luther on the mass is certainly not irrelevant to that passage of time and it is impossible to say how far the Augsburg liturgy has provided motives for heightening or alleviating the judgment.

The interference of external circumstances (in this case his protagonists) is even more evident in the sequence of actions which constitute the Dupuis affair. A first communication of 'contestations' in around a dozen pages clearly stemmed from the publication in Italy of his work on the theology of religions by Queriniana, on which the theologian Inos Biffi passed a negative judgment in *Avvenire*, the daily paper of the Italian conference of bishops.[28] Dupuis replied with 188 pages of clarifications made with a colleague and dated Christmas 1998. The Congregation examined it on 30 June 1999. These pages did not, however, calm the examiners (or some of them); the General of the Society of Jesus was informed of this, together with a 'doctrinal judgment' to which Dupuis replied with 60 pages. However, these were not enough for the Congregation, which decided, with the assent of the pope, to issue the notification, shown to Dupuis on 7 September 2000. However, to take account of the fact that phrases had been imputed to him which he had quoted and criticized, the work had to be redone, despite the papal signature, and a new version was issued on 17 December with a second signature by the pope; Dupuis agreed to fulfil the request to 'account for his own work', but the version issued on 26 January, again signed by the pope, said that he had to 'assent to the theses' of the Congregation. As Cardinal König says, the consistency of the bureaucracy reveals the 'difficulties' of the Congregation;[29] it is therefore impossible not to doubt whether the notification was also issued to respond to the ill-feeling aroused by *Dominus Iesus* and also set out to respond to the dismay of those who asked loudly whether *Dominus Iesus* was not trying to correct of limit the action of John Paul II or others, in Rome and outside it.[30]

It does not seem to me possible to say that something similar has happened in the case of Vidal at a public level: however, the experts can understand whether positions are being taken in moral theology for which the notification against Vidal can serve as a warning (directly or indirectly).[31] What is certain, though, is that the case of the Redemptorist moral theologian shows that beyond the formal scruple which the notifications demonstrate, the time factor constitutes a form of vindictive punishment, deprived of those mechanisms of control and guarantees that the canons ensure on the basis of membership of the church through baptism.[32] The prolongation of the case becomes a form of pressure which is all the stronger, the more the victim is a Catholic who does not know how to remain in suspense as to *his* correct faith and his capacity to serve the truth in the proper condition of the scholar (that is the case with all three scholars in question).

It is enough to state some facts in sequence to justify this statement. The first edition of Vidal's *Moral de actitudes* was published in 1974, the ninth in 1990; it was translated into Italian and published by Cittadella in 1994. After this date, which initiated the examination in the Congregation, the outcome (an official contestation) was communicated to the superior of the Redemptorists on 13 December 1997. Vidal's reply, dated 4 June 1998, took 368 days to be responded to: on 7 June 1999 the Congregation replied, modifying the object of the contention 'by way of exception' and gave the author four months to reply. Vidal's new clarification was delivered in due time and examined on 10 November 1999 by the Congregation which 'thinks it necessary to produce the text of a notification'. This notification was prepared between the evening of 10 November and the morning of 12 November 1999, so that it could be submitted to the Holy Father for approval that Friday morning. The notification was then communicated to Fr Vidal in a meeting which took place six and a half months later, on 2 June 2000. The colloquium was reported to the ordinary session of the Congregation on 12 June 2000 and then again (why?) on 7 February 2001: after that it was again submitted to the Holy Father on 9 February 2001 and published in *L'Osservatore Romano* on 16 May 2001. There were almost four years of a pressure which was obviously experienced by the two parties in different ways: the one who makes the objections about the author never comes into play and remains 'objective' in his anonymity, while the author cannot prevent the dissolution of that fabric of human, scholarly and spiritual relations which form part of his life. To rescue this relational universe he has to accept the solidarity of those who have undergone the same tests (and this may not prove satisfying) or has to accept objections and requests of whatever tone, even contrary to his sense of intellectual rigour. Congar in 1956 described the effect of this disparity in dramatic tones: 'I know that – even if I live another twenty-five or thirty years – I shall never regain either freedom of action or the conditions of normal life. All that I have undertaken, all the preparation of the abundant notes that I have been able to produce up till now, all that is going nowhere and has no future. It is atrocious to be killed alive.' Can this problem be said to have been resolved today?

6. The wearing down of the authorities

Despite this, the role of the conferences of bishops, of the bishops, and of the superior generals, which could diminish such disparity, is little used in practice.

I emphasize the *practical* level, because in principle this is not the case. The *Ratio agendi* of the Congregation recognizes that the guarding of the faith is a 'law/duty' of a 'pastoral kind' which falls to the bishops 'either individually or meeting in particular Councils or in Episcopal Conferences' (*sic*). The Congregation, quite rightly, is recognized not as having a 'right' but a 'duty', which derives from the duty of the Holy See to intervene where the danger for the faith goes beyond the competence of a 'national' conference or a writing has an influence which is 'more than national'. With this formulation it moves back a little, in terms of application, from the pledge to collaborate with the local churches which the last head of the Holy Office, Cardinal Alfredo Ottaviani, had solemnly made in the notification *Per litteras* of 14 June 1966,[33] but does not betray its substance.

However, in the case of translations of books (and specifically in the case of Italian translations which have an impact on a closed theological culture in the pontifical seminaries and faculties, quite often dialogue with the different authorities involved in action and knowledge is intimidating) it is very easy for the Congregation for the Doctrine of Faith to claim its own competence and to evaluate what capacity for dialogue there is between theologians and their ordinaries or superiors. And this is what has happened in the case of Dupuis and Vidal.[34]

Quite apart from realizing – in particular in the last-mentioned case of the Redemptorist moral theologian – that the Congregation risks escalating the conflict boundlessly, the excess of zeal on the part of higher or lower functionaries of the office risks bringing the national episcopates themselves before the tribunal of doctrines as an opposing party.[35] By declaring itself to be a competent organ without any connection with bishops or nuncios, the Congregation first deprives the bishops of a say and then loads on them the weight of decisions which have been taken by those who have not even said a word to fulfil the daily task of keeping open contact with all, out of faithfulness to the gospel which is addressed to all. And that is a problem.

So it is not the case that in the discussion between Vidal and the Congregation the doctrinal commission of the Spanish episcopal conference has been involved in the last phase of the debate and has taken upon itself the task of guaranteeing the fulfilment of the conditions imposed by the notification. The dragging out of a practice which in the first place was suspicious of the bishops prevents the Congregation from confronting an author in advance of the episcopal conference with its consent; but in the end it is proper for a conference to be involved in settling a question which puts their discernment in doubt, especially if the books are by a professor.

It will be said that this principle guarantees the function of the appeal to Rome, but it makes the Congregation (and also 'Ratzinger', as the simplification by the press has it) a catalyst for tensions which are not easy to dissipate and cannot be maintained. Moreover, the *ratio agendi* preserves the ancient custom (associated with the praxis of the Inquisition and the conciliar procedure of the construction of anathemas) of elaborating the charge by lists of 'propositions which are erroneous or are to be condemned'.[36] This exposes quite complex works to distortions which are all the easier to produce, the more the person making the denunciation (who has sometimes been close to the person under suspicion) has malicious intentions. And there are difficulties in an examination which gives the Congregation the power both to accuse and to judge the plausibility of the defence. This is a form of legal rudimentality which Congar did not hesitate to compare with the political policy of totalitarian Nazism: at all events it is a coarseness which is wearing on those who apply it. By refusing to involve the episcopate (in the role of a filter or as a third party), the Congregation is pressed with demands for transparency which it cannot meet. Thus, for Vidal, it is up to the Spanish bishops to function as guarantors, hostages of the correction within a language, a culture, a system of relations which has certainly not been improved or healed by the publication of the notification. Think of the cost of and the friction caused by the concentration of much power and little authority in a system of broad communication, leading to mistrust between episcopates and Roman organs, in the complex climate of church life, and timidity in theological research.

7. The ambiguity

There is another element in the corrective notifications signed by Messner, Dupuis and Vidal which seems to me significant: this is the name given to the offence to be found in the works. These are no longer errors or crimes against the faith, and we no longer have the usual categorizations of the scholastic manuals. In connection with Messner mention is made of the 'fundamental options' which must be recalled 'unequivocally . . . if a theology is to be considered "Catholic"'; and if Messner is charged with being equivocal, the other two authors are accused of 'ambiguity' (Dupuis three times, Vidal eight). This is not an unprecedented *concept* in Roman condemnations: propositions conducive to error, dangerous doctrines, formulae which offend pious ears, can be found in many cases in the history of doctrinal proceedings.[37] The point is that the notification is given when an author in whom errors or imprecisions have been noted has given a reply that the Congregation has thought insufficient. In short, ambiguity is a residual crime, contested by written phrases or phrases that are called for, but one for which the suspected offender is responsible: there is a recognition of the substantial goodness of the explanations, but other levels of communication in the church are evoked to say that these explanations are not enough.

In the case of Dupuis the ambiguity and/or the insufficient explanations are set out by chapters: 'the interpretation of the one and universal saving mediation of Christ, the oneness and fullness of the revelation of Christ, the universal saving action of the Holy Spirit, the ordination of all men to the church, the value and the significance of the saving function of the religions'. The notification gives a very summary account of these, leaving the burden of clarification to the author.[38]

In the case of Vidal it is said that in the examination account has been taken of 'the ambiguities over artificial heterological procreation, therapeutic and eugenic abortion and laws on abortion'; in reality the notification also objects to the way in which Vidal has treated the christological foundation of ethics, homosexuality and autoeroticism. And before that there are strong criticisms (indeed the strongest criticisms) of a failure to accept 'the traditional doctrine on intrinsically evil actions' and on the consequent absoluteness of the prohibitions against them.

Thus the use of the category of ambiguity focusses attention on propositions which, put in sequence, indicate that here there is a problem of theological method, indeed of 'correct theological method'.[39] The correct methodology, which is capable of producing results without the ambiguity complained about, would therefore be that used by the ordinary magisterium – on highly topical and radically new questions like those involved here.[40] The topic of the theology of religions, like the ethical problems associated with the self-understanding of men and women in contemporary society, raises new problems on which the magisterium (with whose pronouncements the Congregation for the Doctrine of Faith regularly agrees) feels called on to intervene, often very rapidly. That risks giving the impression that the correct theological method consists above all in ceasing to look in the depths of Christian tradition, in the exhaustible resources of the word of the Bible, in the wisdom of the people who have the dignity of living simply, for fragments, ideas, analogies or models for the problems arising in situations and forms which are not necessarily those thought of by a magisterium which 'bureaucratically' gives weight to an official opinion that necessarily guarantees the monocular vision of continuity.[41] Demonstrating to all theologians and seminarians, priests and pastors, by means of the 'exemplary' punishment of theologians like Messner, Dupuis or Vidal, who are certainly not refractory or presumptuously independent, amounts to restricting the area in which theology can be practised to a repetition of the ecclesiastical magisterium in all those matters which *a posteriori* will be declared to be relevant to the substance of doctrine. That may perhaps seem more prudent than the risky attempt to discern the thousands of signals in a society which has become so globalized and fragmented, but it does not resolve the ambiguity of a bureaucratization of the truth and threatens the indispensable resource that thought represents for the church.[42]

We can see this clearly in the part of the notification on Vidal which is devoted to the topic of abortion. Vidal, who in his book expounds and comments on the thesis of John Paul II, is judged to be 'ambiguous' in the phrase 'not all legal liberalization of abortion is directly contrary to ethics'. The Congregation imputes to the wording the fact that in this way the reader does not have the 'possibility of determining what kind of laws which decriminalize abortion are considered not directly contradictory to ethics'. The objection raised here is unexceptionable but also banal: the phrase does not say what it does not say – that is clear. But what is the alternative to this presumed ambiguity, and what kind of danger does such ambiguity pose to the Catholic faith?[43] A price has to be paid for linking the level of the truth to that of love, the level of experience to that of doctrine, the level of pastoral tradition to that of the doctrinal magisterium, and there is a risk that all this can be read in the category of ambiguity. However, this can also be a necessary part of life and the unstoppable course of the gospel in time. If it is thought that the bishops are not in a position to cope with these problems, that Christians are immature, that the theologians are incapable of tackling such problems in their thought, is there not a risk of gradually reducing Christian life, theology, the ministry?

Congar's fierce irony recognized that for the guardians of orthodoxy his error had been to tackle problems 'without aligning myself on the one article that they want to impose on the behaviour of all Christianity, which is to think nothing, to say nothing but that there is a pope who thinks everything, who says everything, and the whole quality of being a Catholic consists in obeying him. They wanted to be absolutely the only ones; except in a narrow free sector in inconsequential matters; they simply wanted their *effata* to be repeated and orchestrated, to cries of "Brilliant".'[44] How is it possible to be certain that the psychosis of ambiguity does not hide the very mentality of which the future cardinal complained fifty years ago?

8. The origin of an unfinished debate

These little questions, which are external and marginal, are not in any way intended to indicate that the three notifications which were given every two months from December on did not have a specific content which deserves attention, and which others have expressed elsewhere. Above all the notification against Vidal seems to me to be dominated by a debate on the intrinsically evil act which years ago returned to the theological debate as the core of moral theology and as crucial to the conception of the magisterium and the assent due to its propositions. The debate on the intrinsically evil act did not arise from within the machinery of the Congregation with the writings of Marciano Vidal; it developed well beforehand, from the encyclicals and instructions on the magisterium and assent which have suggested a 'doctrinal policy of the Roman curia' after Vatican II.[45]

A small but instructive dossier which a famous friend, now deceased, had the kindness to make for me a few years ago, allows me to put forward for the use of historians a hypothesis about the moment at which this discussion came to light. This is a fascicle of the Congregation for the Doctrine of Faith from 1986 which brings together opinions and proposals apparently made on an occasional basis, but which have continued to have had an influence to the present day, more through an internal problem of the organs which should have implemented it than for other reasons. In the summer of that year, in an academic discussion with Josef Seifert and Rocco Buttiglione (both of whom were lecturing at the University of Lichtenstein), Franz Böckle had the idea of challenging his opponents by suggesting that they should 'ask the pope' to specify the validity of *Humanae vitae*.[46] Seifert took his adversary at his word and wrote a letter to John Paul II, asking for an infallible definition on the existence of an intrinsically evil acts, like the suppression of an innocent human life, to be applied primarily to abortion. This letter was transmitted by the Secretary of State, Agostino Casaroli, to the Congregation for the Doctrine of the Faith on 17 November 1986. Immediately a dossier came into being with various opinions, very essentialist and prudent, and with quite a broad opinion by the American theologian Germain G. Grisez,[47] taking up Seifert and Buttiglione's preoccupations,[48] he argued that an infallible definition of 'intrinsically evil' acts like the killing of the innocent was necessary, whether for reasons connected with the development of moral theology or to defend the magisterium, the real 'victim' of tendencies in this sector.[49]

The opinions gathered allowed a further consultor, Fr K. Becker SJ, from the Gregorian,[50] to put forward insurmountable objections to the requests for a dogmatic definition on the matter. Becker, with a rigorously scholastic method and language, distinguished between the spheres in which it was possible to 'define' and noted that Vatican I had had no intention of inserting the *moralia naturalia* in the heritage of the *fide divina tenendum*; he then demonstrated that the 'narrow object' of the question raised by the philosophers had not been clarified, and demonstrated how it would be impossible to arrive at certainty on the type of assent required by the magisterium in a dogmatic definition *in lege morali naturali* (where dogmatics justifies itself 'only to avoid the misunderstanding of scientific definition').[51] Moreover Becker rejected the idea that it was possible to arrive at such a definition, also in deference to the fact that the number of Catholics 'incapable of living in a time of transition with its crises and disorders' had increased. To defend such less well-trained Catholics by narrow dogmatizing would have meant 'leaning on a definition with a grave defect'. Becker's option, which accepted from Grisez only the advice to hold a colloquium in the Theological Commission, was followed in the dossier by the proposal for an instruction 'On Some Fundamental Questions of Moral Theology', but along the lines of the thesis of Seifert, Buttiglione and Grisez. As we know, this then had an echo in *Evangelium vitae*, in which there is a formula on abortion as a grave moral disorder which appeals to the charisma of infallibility,[52] but remains limited (this was very much thanks to Cardinal Ratzinger) to a very small object.[53] Thus an unsatisfied demand expressed in the attempts to broaden the area of the definitive magisterium which took place in the 1990s[54] (Seifert's motion was only the indication) returned in the notification on Vidal and will perhaps appear in other circumstances.

9. One last question

So glimpses of a complex reality emerge in the notifications. There are the old contradictions of a church which wants to repent of the errors made in the name of the gospel but does not know how to reform the institutions which have committed them. There are the traces of differences within the Congregation, which are compensated for – I am still speaking in terms of the political logic of organization, not of theological content – by unloading on the outside world whatever cannot be clarified inside. There are the signs of that cult of the precedent which is at the heart of the whole practice of the Roman curia and that form of bureaucratic collegiality (so that a prefect has to respect the clergy and the religious which he has around him more than the bishops whom he does not often meet), which form part of a culture of government of the Latin church that has survived and is still waiting to find the right counterbalances.

These are the ordinary dynamics of any organization made up of real people with different histories: ordinary dynamics, but dynamics which affect real people. By their nature the notifications relate to books, but they certainly affect people's sensitivities, their dignity and perhaps their rights. And beyond that authors are caught up in a web of suspicions, and then there are all the people who, impelled by the clamour generated by the Roman past, catch themselves thinking the same thing. How many of them, in the name of faithfulness, are spurred on to a intellectual acquiescence, to an unintentional weakness for which they pay the price when it proves that Catholics are extremely vulnerable when confronted with the simplistic, depersonalizing and inhuman ethical and spiritual models of the sects?

Is it wise to do away with the awareness that the problems about which theology is asking today are being carried around in many hearts, in many experiences and in many different cultures? Those who face these difficult questions, whether they are laity or priests, bishops or cardinals or others, from whatever perspective, need something more than an updated *Index librorum ambiguorum*, provided on the website www.vatican.va, despite the decisions of 1966. Would anyone want to revive that repressive instrument, as a service to the church, after twenty years of a pontificate which has made a style of government out of the 'ambiguity' of gestures and words? And if it does not serve the church as a whole, whom does it benefit?

Translated by John Bowden

Notes

1. It is public knowledge that the work *Jesus, Symbol of God*, by Roger Haight, which was given the Catholic Press Association Award in the USA in 1999, is currently under examination. Authoritative and important organs have intervened over this procedure, including the *National Catholic Reporter* and *America*. However, almost popular works (like the little pastoral book on miracles, *Wunder. Eine existenzielle Auslegung*, by Fr Josef Imbach, published in 1997), have also been the object of the Congregation's attention. With candid Franciscan wit Fr Imbach has replied, as requested, to the objections made against him in a short article, 'Joseph contra Joseph', which appeared in the monthly *Kirche Intern*, 10/2000. In it he asks the Cardinal Prefect of the Congregation to get an expert opinion on the experts who have accused *Wunder*.

2. One thinks of the vicissitudes of Tissa Balasuriya, who was excommunicated on 2 January 1997 and readmitted to communion after subscribing to Paul VI's 'credo', cf. *Il Regno- attualità* 43, 1998, p.87. It would be useful to construct an exhaustive map of the doctrinal conflicts in the post-conciliar church to discover the areas in which the local authority effectively guarantees control and freedom.

3. There is no study of the disputes between Kasper and Ratzinger on the universal church and the particular church; similarly, there has been no analysis of the statements of the Rota under Cardinal Pompedda, in which there is an emphasis on human reality in the legal analysis of behaviour which is very different from that used in certain theological abstractions on bioethical problems.

4. Cf. E. Poulat, 'La théologie trois fois déstabilisée', *Revue d'éthique et de théologie morale. Le supplement*, 1998, no. 207, pp.125–37.

5. Cf. A. Prosperi, 'Tribunali della coscienza. Inquisitori, confessori, missionari', Turin 1996, pp.135–53: 137. This is based on M. Firpo and D. Marcatto, *Il processo inquisitoriale del cardinal Morone* (3 vols), Rome 1981–89; Giuseppe De Luca could survey the Pole process (cf. Prosperi, p.136n.) for a work which was never completed.

6. This is the shrewd theme of E. Brambila, *Alle origini del Sant'Uffizio. Penitenza, confessione e giustizia spirituale dal medioevo al XVI secolo*, Bologna 2000.

7. For the origin of the *Professio fidei tridentina* in the sphere of the Inquisition see H. Jedin, 'Zur Enstehung der *Professio fidei Tridentina*', in *Annuarium Historiae Conciliorum* 6, 1974, pp.369–75; for the developments see D. Menozzi, 'La professione di fede del "*motu proprio*" [*Ad tuendam fidem*] in una prospettiva storica', *Cristianesimo nella storia* 21, 2000, pp.7–35.

8. Cf. S. Pagano, *Comunicazione, al congresso su Pio X tenuta a Vicenza nel 2001*, and G. Vian, *La riforma della chiesa per la restaurazione cristiana della società* (2 vols), Rome 1998.

9. E. Poulat, *Intégrisme et catholicisme intégral. Un réseau secret international antimoderniste: La Sapinère (1909–1921)*, Tournai 1969.

10. Cf. P. Colin, *L'audace et le soupçon: la crise dans le catholicisme français 1893–1914*, Paris 1997, and Christoph Théobald, 'De Vatican I aux années 1950: révélation, foi et raison, inspiration, dogme et magistère infaillible', in *La parole du salut. Histoire des dogmes IV*, Paris 1996, pp.227–470.

11. E. Fouilloux, *La collection 'Sources Chrétiennes'. Éditer les Pères de l'église au XXe siècle*, Paris 1995, and the proceedings of the Toulouse colloquium 'Surnaturel. Une controverse au coeur du thomisme zu XXe siècle', *Revue Thomiste* 109, 2001, pp.101/2.

12. E. Fouilloux, *Une église en quête de liberté: la pensée catholique française entre modernisme et Vatican II*, Paris 1998, and *Au coeur du XXe siècle religieux*, Paris 1993.

13. Y. Congar, *Journal d'un théologien 1946–1956*, edited with an introduction by E. Fouilloux, Paris 2000.

14. Cf. A. Riccardi, *Il potere del papa da Pio XII a Giovanni Paolo II*, Rome and Bari 1993, pp.289–300.

15. Cf. in *Storia del concilio Vaticano II diretta da Giuseppe Alberigo, vol.3, Il concilio adulto. Il secondo periodo e la seconda intersessione (settembre 1963–settembre 1964)*, Bologna 1998, pp.141–53.

16. Cf. G. Ruggieri, 'La politica dottrinale della curia romana nel postconcilio', *Cristianesimo nella storia* 21, 2000, pp.103–31.

17. For the figure of the first post-conciliar prefect see Franjo Seper, *grada za zivotopis*, and his speeches at the Council (*Interventi na II. vatikanskom koncilu*) and the offical proceedings (*Dokumenti Sv. congregacije za nauk vjere*, 1968–81) (2 vols), Zagreb 1983. For the opinions of Ratzinger at the time he took office cf. B. Mondin, *Problemi e compiti della Chiesa oggi secondo Ratzinger, Congar, Moltmann e Cullmann* [extract], Brescia 1980; and afterwards his interview with V. Messori, *Vittorio Messori a colloquio con il cardinal Raztinger. Rapporto sulla fede*, Turin 1985; A. Nichols, *The Theology of Joseph Ratzinger, An Introductory Study*, Edinburgh 1988, and now J. L. Allen Jr, *Cardinal Ratzinger. The Vatican's Enforcer of the Faith*, New York 2001.

18. These have been collected in two volumes as *Congregazione: Documenta inde a concilio Vaticano II expleto edita (1966–1985)*, Vatican City 1995; *Dall' 'Inter insigniores' all' 'Ordinatio sacerdotalis'. Documenti e commenti*, Vatican City 1996. The Libreria Editrice Vaticana has continued to publish the proceedings of the Congregation in fascicles, but these have not yet been brought together for the last five years.

19. The rule contained an important variation on the penal regime of the church established there (art. 28), namely that 'whenever the author has not corrected the errors indicated in a satisfactory way and with adequate publicity, and the Ordinary Session has come to the conclusion that he is involved in the crime of heresy, apostasy or schism, the Congregation will proceed to declare the penalties incurred *latae sententiae*; no recourse is allowed against such a declaration.' John Paul II has verbally approved this article (and also no. 29) despite arguments against it: to accuse the suspect of negligence in giving 'adequate publicity' to his own submission and to use this as a cause for a condemnation against which there is no recourse opens the door to an uncertainty which cannot easily be resolved, the scope of which it is not easy to discover.

20. For the problem of the profession of faith and its links with *CJC* see A. Monti, *L'obligo di emettere la professione di fede. Studio teologico-giuridico del. can. 833*, Rome 1998; cf. H. Schmitz, '"Professio fidei" und "Iusiurandum fidelitatis". Glaubensbekenntnis und Treueid. Wiederbelebung des Antimodernisten-eides?', *Archiv für katholisches Kirchenrecht* 57, 1988, pp.353–429 (it did not appear until 1990). For the *motu proprio Ad tuendam fidem* cf. the contributions collected in the fascicle 'Disciplinare la verità?', ed. G. Ruggieri, *Cristianesimo nella storia* 21, 2000, pp.1–258; B. Sesboué, 'À propos du *motu proprio* de Jean-Paul II *Ad tuendam fidem*', *Études* 10, 1998, no. 3894, pp.357–67; J. P. Durand, 'À propos d'un decision de Jean-Paul II, *Ad tuendam fidem*', *Revue d'éthique et de théologie morale, Le supplement, La vie et la science III-VII*; L. Örsy, 'Von der Autorität kirchlicher Dokumente. Eine Fallstudie zum Apostolischen Schreiben *Ad tuendam fidem*', *Stimmen der Zeit* 216, 1998, pp.735–40. This gave rise to a dispute with J. Ratzinger, also in *Stimmen der Zeit* 217, 1999, pp.169–71, 305–16. Cf. also H. J. Pottmeyer, 'Auf fehlbare Weise unfehlbar? Zu einer neuen Form päpstlichen Lehrens?', *Stimmen der Zeit* 217, 1999, pp.233–42; summed up by B. E. Ferme, '*Ad tuendam fidem*: Some Reflections', in *Periodica de re morali et canonica* 88, 1999, pp.579–606. For the other important actions in which the Congregation has had the role of author or inspirer cf. A. Antón, 'I teologi davanti all'istruzione "*Donum veritatis*". Il compito del teologo tra "ecclesialità e scientificità" e il suo rapporto col magistero ecclesiastico', *Gregorianum* 78.2, 1997, pp.223–65, and P. Eyt, 'La portée théologique du mot "definitive"', in *Trois notes sur magistère et morale*, Documents épiscopat 1990, no. 16, pp.5–7; H. McSorley, 'Ecclesial Communion, Reception and the Apostolic Letter of Pope John Paul II "*Ordinatio sacerdotalis*"', in *Communion et*

réunion. Mélanges Jean-Marie Roger Tillard, ed. G. R. Evans and M. Gourgues, Louvain 1995, 389–401. Cf. F. A. Sullivan, 'Secondary Object of Infallibility', *Theological Studies* 45, 1993, pp.536–50, 93–94 and now J. F. Chiron, *L'infaillibilité et son objet. L'autorité du magistère infaillible de l'église s'étend-elle aux vérités non révélés?*, Paris 1999; N. Lüdecke, *Die Grundnormen des katholischen Lehrrechts in den päpstlichen Gesetzbüchern und neueren Äusserungen in päpstlicher Autorität*, Würzburg 1997.

21. Cf. Y. Congar, 'Après "Infaillible" de Hans Küng: Bilan et discussion', *Revue de Sciences Philosophiques et Théologiques* 58, 1974, pp.243–52, and A. Hontañón, *La doctrina acerca de la infalibilidad a partir de la declaración Mysterium ecclesiae* (1973), Pamplona 1998.

22. The notification on the volume *Church, Charism and Power* issued on 11 March 1985, cf. *Documenta* (n.18), pp.286–93.

23. *AAS* 79, 1987, and *Documenta* (n.18).

24. Cf. E. Brambila, 'Confessione, casi riservati e giustizia "spirituale" dal XV secolo al concilio di Trento: i reati di fede e di morale', in *Fonti ecclesiastiche per la storia sociale e religiosa d'Europa: XV-XVIII secolo*, ed. C. Nubola and A. Turcini, Bologna 1999, pp.491–540: 499.

25. Congar, *Journal* (n.13), p. 427.

26. Cf. F. König, 'Let the Spirit Breathe', *The Tablet*, 7 April 2001, pp.483–4.

27. Cf. A. Maffeis, *La giustificazione. Percorsi teologici nel dialogo tra le Chiese*, Cinisello Balsamo 1998, and *Dossier sulla giustificazione. La dichiarazione congiunta cattolico-luterana. Commento e dibattito teologico*, ed. A Maffeis, Brescia 2000.

28. There is a report on www.adista.it

29. Cf. König, 'Spirit' (n.26), 484, and again his observations to V. Prisciandaro, 'Una chiesa a porte aperte', in *Jesus*, 1001, no.5: '*Dominus Iesus* does not cite a book or an author but in fact was published while the notification against Fr Dupuis' volume was being prepared. In short, it seems that religious pluralism is positive for the pope but is problematical for the Congregation for the Doctrine of Faith. It is also a fact which has left me perplexed. Three versions of the notification against Dupuis have been produced, all already with the pope's confirmation. What is the significance of the fact that the pope confirms a different text three times? It seems to me that this story demonstrates the difficulties which the procedure of the Congregation encounters. As for theological research, in my view the field needs to be left open for discussion. I understand that the task of the Congregation is not easy, but there is a need to be attentive and not to return to old systems.'

30. For the theological debate cf. C. van Wijnbergen, 'Reactions to *Dominus Iesus* in the German-Speaking World', *Concilium* 2001/3, pp.147–52, and *Dominus Iesus. Anstössige Wahrheit oder anstössige Kirche? Dokumente, Hintergründe, Standpunkte und Folgerungen*, ed. M. J. Rainer, Münster 2001. *Civiltà Cattolica*

151, 2000 expressed reservations about Dupuis with a procedure which during the modernist crisis or during the repression of the *nouvelle théologie* was often thought enough to admonish the suspect and to suspend public proceedings by the Holy Office; the reasons for this function of review with respect to the Holy See are illustrated in the presentation of the history of the paper in www.laciviltacattolica.it; for its role at the beginning of the century see G. Sale, *La Civiltà Cattolica nella crisi modernista (1900–1907), fra intransigentismo politico e integralismo dottrinale*, Milan 2001.

31. D. Tettamanzi, *La nuova bioetica cristiana*, Casale Monferrato 2000, appeared during the jubilee year; it was reviewed by F. Cultera in *Civiltà Cattolica* 152, 2001, II, no. 621, pp.254–62.

32. Cf. E. Corecco, 'Ius et communio', in *Scritti di diritto canonica*, ed. G. Borgonovo and A. Cattaneo, vol.2, Asti 1997, pp.617–718.

33. *Per litteras* removed the status of ecclesiastical law from the Index of Prohibited Books. For the half step backwards constituted by the letter *Cum Oecumenicum* of 20 July 1966, which exhorted the ordinaries on the errors of the conciliar hermeneutic, cf. *Informations catholiques internationales* 278, 1966, p.5.

34. In the case of Messner the Bishop of Innsbruck performed a modest bureaucratic role with no public explanation of how and when a dissertation could constitute a threat to the universal church.

35. Something similar happened, with very different outcomes, when in 1993 the three bishops of Upper Rhineland, Oskar Saier of Freiburg, Walter Kasper of Rottenburg and Karl Lehmann of Mainz, tried to find a way not to exclude remarried divorced persons from the eucharist. This provoked a brusque reaction from Ratzinger, who called on them to drop their position (*Schreiben an die Bischöfe der Katholischen Kirche über den Kommunionempfang von Wieder-verheiraten Geschiedenen Gläubigen*, Vatican City 1994); the question, with no names mentioned, returns in Ratzinger's preface to the anthology *Sulla pastorale dei divorziati*, Vatican City 1998.

36. For the formulation of anathematization in conciliar history cf. P. Fransen, 'Réflexions sur l'anathème au Concile de Trente', *Ephemerides Theologicae Lovanienses* 29, 1953, now in id., *Hermeneutics of the Councils and Other Studies*, Louvain 1985.

37. Cf. the manual by Benedicto Ojetti, *Synopsis rerum moralium et iuris pontificis . . . Editio tertia et emendata*, Rome 1909.

38. An article by me on this is forthcoming.

39. The singular is a typical feature of a nineteenth-century debate; cf. G. A. McCool, *Catholic Theology in the Nineteenth Century: The Quest for a Unitary Method*, New York 1977.

40. Cf. F. A. Sullivan, *Creative Fidelity: Weighing and Interpreting Documents of the Magisterium*, New York 1966.

41. Cf. D. Tracy, 'The Uneasy Alliance Reconceived: Catholic Theological

Method, Modernity and Postmodernity', *Theological Studies* 50, 1989, pp.548–70.

42. The unsigned article which accompanies the notification on Vidal (it is hard to see why it forms part of the acts of the Congregation on the collection on the website www.vatican.va) seeks to tackle this question, but with contradictory outcomes; it accepts a 'patience of maturation', conscious of the tensions between magisterium and theology in the 1950s, which must be common to all, whereas in n. 4 there is emphasis on the fact that such patience is required only of theologians, in conformity with what is required by the instruction *Donum veritatis*. Cf also a critical position on Vidal in P. Carlotti, *Teologia morale e magistero. Documenti pontifici recenti*, Rome 1997.

43. As well as different perspectives other ambiguities could be collected and a sterile dispute could be opened on what is more ambiguous. Thus someone will say that J. Ratzinger's work *Lo spirito della liturgia*, Cinisello Balsamo 2000, which quotes the liturgical constitution *Sacrosanctum Concilium* only once in passing, could convince readers that as a theologian he seeks to diminish the scope of a conciliar deliberation; or, as the Italian press has done maliciously, someone will find it ambiguous that in May 2001 Carindal Camillo Ruini, for reasons connected with the formation of the government after the right-wing victory in the election, had to correct his collaborators and state that 'the bishops did not make any particular request for the revision or modification of law 194 (which legalizes abortion)'. www.chiesacattolica.it/sir, note of 18 May 2001, pp.15:25.

44. Congar, *Journal* (n.13), p.425.

45. Cf. G. Ruggieri, 'La politica dottrinale della curia romana nel postconcilio', in *Cristianesimo nella storia* 21, 2000, pp.103–31.

46. See his *Fundamantalmoral*, Munich [4]1985; in 1986 Böckle had edited *Concilium* 100 on sexuality in contemporary Catholicism (extracts are being posted on www.concilium.org/fran.htm),

47. The Georgetown scholar had written *Contraception and the Natural Law*, Milwaukee 1964, and *Abortion: the Myths, the Realities and the Arguments*, New York 1972 (which even in the index makes a connection between Luther's doctrine of justification and the negation of intrinsically evil acts).

48. That was his position at the time of his contribution to *Persona, verità e morale. Atti del congresso internazionale di teologia morale* (1986), Rome 1988, pp.497–511.

49. This sensation emerges several times in the contributions collected from the Lateran University in *Humanae vitae: vent'anni dopo. Atti del congresso internazionale di teologia morale (1988)*, Treviglio 1989, which includes articles by Grisez and Seifert.

50. I presume Fr Karl J. Becker, author in 1942 of the PUG thesis *Die Rechtfertigungslehre nach Domingo de Soto, das Denken eines Konzilsteilnehmers vor, in*

und nach Trient, and the dispensation issued in 1980 in the faculty where he had then been teaching on the general history of baptism.

51. For the preconciliar positions see H.-J. Pottmeyer, *Unfehlbarkeit und Souveränitat. Die päpstliche Unfehlbarkeit im System der Ultramontanen Ekklesiologie des 19. Jahrhundert*, Mainz 1976; for the Council see K. Schatz, *Vatikanum I, 1869–1870*, Munich 1992.

52. Cf. Chiron, *L'infaillibilité* (n.20), and still G. Thils, *L'infaillibilité pontificale. Sources – conditions – limites*, Gembloux 1968.

53. The comments of cardinals and ecclesiastics which appeared in *L'Osservatore romano* are collected in *Pontificia Academia Pro Vita* – Evangelium vitae *di Sua Santità Giovanni Paolo II. Enciclica e Commenti*, Vatican City 1995; *The symposium* Evangelium vitae *e diritto*, ed. A. López Trujillo, J. Herranz and E. Sgreccia, Vatican City 1997; *Pontificia Academia Pro Vita – Evangelium vitae. Five Years of Confrontation with the Society*, ed. J. de D. Vial Correa and E. Sgreccia, Vatican City 2001.

54. See my 'Definitivus/definitive', *Cristianesimo nella storia* 21, 2000, pp.171–205.

Contributors

EVELYN A. KIRKLEY specializes in the religious history of the United States from the pre-colonial era to the present. Her work includes Native American, African American, Catholic, Protestant, Jewish, and sectarian religious communities as well as cultural and civil religion. Her area of concentration is the late nineteenth century, particularly issues of race, class, gender, and sexuality among non-mainstream religious groups.

Address: University of San Diego, Department of Theology and Religious Studies, 5998 Alcala Park, San Diego, CA 92110
E-mail: ekirkley@sandiego.edu

ANN-CATHRIN JARL gained her doctorate in ethics at the faculty of theology of the University of Uppsala with a thesis on feminist economic ethics, and now teaches ethics in the faculty. In 1995 she was named woman economist of the year, winning the annual prize awarded by the Föreningsbanken. She has been secretary for the project of economic ethics in theology directed by Carl-Heinrich Grenholm, and has been in charge of the section on feminist perspectives. She has written *Women and Economic Justice: Ethics in Feminist Liberation Theology and Feminist Economics*, Uppsala 2000, and is president of the Swedish section of the International League of Women for Peace and Freedom.

Address: Svartbäcksg. 46 J, 75333 Uppsala, Sweden
E-mail: Ann-Cathrin.Jarl@teo.uu.se

RHACEL SALAZAR PARREÑAS is Ford Foundation Postdoctoral Fellow (2001–2002) and Assistant Professor of Women's Studies and Asian American Studies at the University of Wisconsin, Madison. She is the author of *Servants of Globalization: Women, Migration, and Domestic Work* (2001) as well as articles that have appeared in *Signs*, *Gender and Society*, and *Feminist Studies*.

Address: University of Wisconsin, Madison, USA
E-mail: rparrenas@facstaff.wisc.edu; rparrenas@hotmail.com

VIRGINIA VARGAS is a Peruvian sociologist and researcher and founder of the Centro de la Mujer Peruana Flora Tristán. She is recognized in Latin America as a pioneer and prominent co-founder of contemporary critical feminism. She was co-ordinator of the non-governmental agencies of Latin America and the Caribbean at the Fourth World Conference on Women at Beijing in 1995. Between 1996 and 2000 she was a member of the Advisory Council to the World Bank. She has been recognized for her intense work for the rights of the poor and women by being awarded distinguished prizes. She has written *El Aporte de la Rebeldia de las Mujeres* (1989) and edited *Caminos a Beijing*, a report on the Beijing conference. She is also the author of many analytical articles on feminism in Peru, Latin America and all over the world.

Address: Centro de la Mujer Peruana Flora Tristán, Parque Hernan Velarde 42, Lima 1, Peru.
E-mail: vargas@amauta.rcp.net.pe

MARIA JOSÉ ROSADO-NUNES is a Brazilian sociologist, with a doctorate in social studies from the École des Hautes Études in Paris. She has worked with and studied base communities in various parts of Brazil. She currently teaches sociology of religion and gender studies on religion at the Pontifical Catholic University of São Paulo (PUC/SP). She is co-founder and co-director of Catholics to the Right to Decide in Brazil. She is the author of *Vida Religiosa nos Meios Populares* (Vozes). Her numerous articles include: 'Irreducible Multiplicity and the Search for a Common Project: A Feminist Perspective', in *Liberation Theologies on Shifting Grounds*, ed. G. de Schrijver, Leuven University Press 1998; 'Women, Family and Catholicism in Brazil: The Issue of Power', in *Family, Religion and Social Change in Diverse Societies* ed. Houseknecht and Pankhurst, Oxford University Press 2000; '"Religions' in *Dictionnaire Critique du Féminisme*, PUF' 2000.

Address: Pontifícia Universidade Católica, Rua Monte Alegre, 984 – Pos, 05014–901 São Paulo /SP – Brasil
E-mail: mjrosado@terra.com.br; mjrosado@pucsp.br

MARGARITA PINTOS DE CEA-NAHARRO was born in Madrid in 1947. A feminist theologian, she is professor of Castilian and ecumenical history and theology in the German School in Madrid; she is also a visiting professor at the University Carlos III and director of the seminar on feminist theology. She works with women's groups, groups of religious and spirituality groups. Her publications include: *La mujer en la iglesia* and *Mujeres y hombres en la construcción del pensamiento occidental.* She has also written a number of articles and contributed to composite works.

Address: Ginzo de Limia, 55, 1° B, 28034 Madrid, Spain
E-mail: margaritapi@mi.madritel.es

ISABELLE BARKER is a doctoral candidate in the Department of Political Science, Rutgers University. She is currently working on a dissertation concerning illegal labour migration and political theories of democracy and the nation-state.

Address: 302 Sixth Street, Brooklyn, NY 11215, USA
E-mail: ivb@rci.rutgers.edu

JASBIR KAUR PUAR is Assistant Professor of Women's Studies and Geography at Rutgers University. She received her PhD in Ethnic Studies from the University of California at Berkeley in 1999. Her recent publications include: 'Global Circuits: Transnational Sexualities and Trinidad', *Signs* (26: 4, 2001); 'Transnational Configurations of Desire: The Nation and its White Closets' (in Matt Wray et al (eds), *The Making and Unmaking of Whiteness*, Durham: Duke University Press 2001) and 'Transnational Sexualities: South Asian Trans/Nationalisms and Queer Diasporas' (in David Eng and Alice Hom (eds), *Q&A: Queer in Asian America*, Philadelphia: Temple University Press 1998: pp.405–22.) As a 1999–2000 Rockefeller Postdoctoral Fellow at the Center for Lesbian and Gay Studies at CUNY she began researching the gay and lesbian tourism industry, and she recently guest edited a special issue of *GLQ* entitled 'Queer Tourism: Geographies of Globalization' (8:1–2, 2002). She also has articles forthcoming in *Antipode: A Radical Journal of Geography* and *Social Text*.

Address: 162 Ryders Lane, Douglass Campus, Rutgers University, New Brunswick, NJ 08901, USA
E-mail: jpuar@rci.rutgers.edu

MARCELLA MARIA ALTHAUS-REID is an Argentinian materialist theologian who works in the area of Queer and Political theologies. She is a Senior Lecturer in Christian Ethics and Systematic theology in the University of Edinburgh, Scotland, where she teaches Feminist Theology and Theology and Globalization. She obtained her Bachelor in Theology from ISEDET, Buenos Aires, and her PhD from St Andrews University, Scotland. Prior to studying for her doctorate she was co-ordinator of a conscientization process in deprived areas of Dundee and Perth. She is a member of the Association of European Women in Theological Research and is on the Feminist Advisory Board for *Concilium*. Together with Professor Lisa Isherwood, she is the executive director for the series 'Queering Theology' for Routledge, London. She is author of *Indecent Theology. Theological Perversions on Sex, Gender and Politics*, London: Routledge 2000.

Address: Faculty of Divinity, New College, The University of Edinburgh, Mound Place, Edinburgh EH1 2LX, Scotland
E-mail: Althausm@div.ed.ac.uk

LIEVE TROCH was born in 1949. She is Belgian and lives in the Netherlands, where she is working as a systematic theologian at the theological faculty in Nijmegen. She is also a professor at the Ecumenical Institute for Religious Sciences in Sao Paulo, Brazil, and is visiting professor in several Asian countries. She has written various articles and edited a number of books on feminist fundamental theology. She has also written *Verzet is het geheim van de vreugde. Fundamentaaltheologische thema's in een feministische discussie* (1996). At present she is investigating inter-faith and inter-cultural work as a feminist theologian.

Address: Min.Nelissenstraat 19, 24818 HS Breda, Netherlands
E-mail: l.troch@theol.kun.nl

MARGARET SHANTHI STEPHENS holds a PhD in theology and is an activist feminist. She is director of the Women's Studies Center, Dindiugl, Talminadu, South India, and national convenor of the Forum of Religious for Justice and Peace. She pioneered the women's theological forum WORTH and is an EATWOT member.

Address: St. Joseph's Hospital, Dindigul 624001, Mannar Thirmalai District, Talminadu, India
E-mail: shanthiwsc@yahoo.com

ALBERTO MELLONI has a degree in history from the University of Bologna and a PhD in Religious History. He was Visiting Fellow in the Department of History at the Catholic University in Fribourg, and has been teaching at the University of Rome since 1994. He is a member of the Institute of Religious Studies, on the Boards of the John XXIII Foundation for Religious Studies, Bologna and of 'Cristianesimo nella storia', acts as Director of the School for PhD students and Director of the Dossetti Library. He has published sources and studies on John XXIII (A.G. Roncalli-Giovanni XXIII, *Il giornale dell'Anima*, Bologna 1987; *Tra Istanbul, Atene e la guerra. A. G. Roncalli vicario e delegato apostolico 1935–1944*, Genova 1993; *La predicazione ad Istanbul*, Firenze 1994). He is the editor of the Italian edition of the History of the Second Vatican Council and editor of some volumes of proceedings of international conferences held in Rome, Moscow, Bologna and Strasbourg (*L'alterità*, with Gianni La Bella, Bologna 1994; *Vatican II at Moscow*, Louvain 1996; *L'evento e le decisioni. Studi sulle dinamiche del concilio Vaticano II*, Bologna 1997; *Experience and intermediate bodies at Vatican II*, Louvain 1999; *I volti della fine del concilio*, Bologna 2000).

Address: Via Crispi 6, I-42100 Reggio Emilia, Italy
E-mail: mlllrt@tin.it; Alberto.melloni@tin.it

Concilium Subscription Information

Issues published in 2002

February 2002/1: *The Many Voices of the Bible*
Edited by Seán Freyne and Ellen van Wolde

April 2002/2: *The Body and Religion*
Edited by Regina Ammicht-Quinn and Elsa Tamez

June 2002/3: *Brazil*
Edited by José Oscar Beozzo and Luiz Carlos Susin

October 2002/4: *Religious Education of Boys and Girls*
Edited by Werner Jeanrond and Lisa Sowle Cahill

December 2002/5: *The Rights of Women*
Edited by The Concilium Foundation

New subscribers: to receive Concilium 2002 (five issues) anywhere in the world, please copy this form, complete it in block capitals and send it with your payment to the address below.

Please enter my subscription for Concilium 2002

☐ Individual **£25.00**/*US$50.00*   ☐ Institutional **£35.00**/*US$75.00*

Issues are sent by air to the USA; please add £10/US$20 for airmail dispatch to all other countries (outside Europe).

☐ I enclose a cheque payable to SCM-Canterbury Press Ltd for £/$ ....

☐ Please charge my MasterCard/Visa   Expires ....

........................../.............................../............................./..............................

Signature ....

Name/Institution ....

Address ....

....

....

Telephone ....

Concilium SCM Press 9–17 St Albans Place London N1 0NX England
Telephone (44) 20 7359 8033 Fax (44) 20 7359 0049
E-mail: scmpress@btinternet.com

DATE DUE

Demco, Inc. 38-293